Cambridge Primary

Hodder Cambridge Primary

English

Learner's Book
Stage 4

Rachel Axten-Higgs

Series Editor: Moira Brown

HODDER
EDUCATION
AN HACHETTE UK COMPANY

The Publishers would like to thank the following for permission to reproduce copyright material:

Photographic acknowledgments
p.4, 'Facts About Bats' from Batworlds, http://www.batworlds.com/

Acknowledgements
p22, p31, *The Happy Alien* copyright © 2004 by Jean Ure, reproduced by kind permission of Jean Ure c/o Caroline Sheldon Literary Agency Ltd; p22, p31, *The Leopard* by Ruskin Bond from *The Story Shop* by Nikki Gamble (published by Hodder Children's Books); p22, 29, from *Escape from Pompeii* by Christina Bailit, published by Frances Lincoln Ltd copyright © 2005, reproduced by permission of Frances Lincoln Ltd; p22, 31, from *Why the Whales Came* by Michael Morpurgo, text copyright © 1985 Michael Morpurgo, published by Egmont UK Ltd and used with permission; p24, from *Ali Baba and Other Stories* from *First Aid Reader B: Ali Baba and Other Stories* (published by Hodder Education); p38, 40, 135, extracts from *The Works 4* compiled by Gaby Morgan and Pie Corbett (published by Macmillan) copyright © the individual authors; p40, *Haiku* by Rachel Axton-Higgs, reproduced by permission of the author; p44, *Angus Miller* is used by permission of the author Pamela Mordecai; p46, *The Sprat and the Jackfish* by Grace Walker Gordon, Pearson Education; p48, from *The Case of the Feathered Mask* by Holly Webb published by Stripes Published and reproduced by permission; p68, "The Three Farmers" from FANTASTIC MR. FOX by Roald Dahl, text copyright © 1981 by Roald Dahl Nominee Limited. Used by permission of Alfred A. Knopf, an imprint of Random House Children's Books, a division of Penguin Random House LLC. All rights reserved; p.74, excerpt from *Over Sea, Under Stone* by Susan Cooper. Copyright © 1965, renewed 1993 by Susan Cooper. Reprinted by permission of Houghton Mifflin Harcourt Publishing Company. All rights reserved; p74, reprinted by permission of HarperCollins Publishers Ltd © 2001 Dianna Wynne Jones; p84–5, *All for a Paisa, an Indian folk tale* by Elaine L. Lindy and adapted as a playscript by Linsay Parker; p88, extract adapted from *Folktales on Stage: Children's Plays for Reader's Theatre* by Aaron Shephard; p94, "Grandma" from GEORGE'S MARVELLOUS MEDICINE by Roald Dahl, text copyright © 1981 by Roald Dahl Nominee Limited. Used by permission of Alfred A. Knopf, an imprint of Random House Children's Books, a division of Penguin Random House LLC. All rights reserved; p99, *The Swimming Lesson* by Madhur Jaffrey © Madhur Jaffrey, reproduced by permission of the author c/o Rogers, Coleridge and White; p102, *Stone Soup* from *Caribbean Comprehension: an integrated, skills-based approach, Book Two*, published by Hodder Education; p106, from *Sam's Duck* by Michael Morpurgo published by HarperCollins and reproduced by permission; p120, *Ali Baba and the Forty Thieves* from *Ali Baba and Other Stories* published by Hodder Education; p129, *Looking at Your Bones* from *Caribbean Comprehension: An integrated, skills-based approach, Book Two*, published by Hodder Education; p140, from *The Secret Dinosaur* by N.S. Blackman, published by Dinosaur Books Ltd, reproduced by permission of Dinosaur Books Ltd.

Every effort has been made to trace all copyright holders, but if any have been inadvertently overlooked the Publishers will be pleased to make the necessary arrangements at the first opportunity.

Practice Test exam-style questions and sample answers are written by the author.

Although every effort has been made to ensure that website addresses are correct at time of going to press, Hodder Education cannot be held responsible for the content of any website mentioned in this book. It is sometimes possible to find a relocated web page by typing in the address of the home page for a website in the URL window of your browser.

Hachette UK's policy is to use papers that are natural, renewable and recyclable products and made from wood grown in sustainable forests. The logging and manufacturing processes are expected to conform to the environmental regulations of the country of origin.

Orders: please contact Bookpoint Ltd, 130 Milton Park, Abingdon, Oxon OX14 4SB. Telephone: +44 (0)1235 827720. Fax: +44 (0)1235 400454. Lines are open 9.00a.m.–5.00p.m., Monday to Saturday, with a 24-hour message answering service. Visit our website at www.hoddereducation.com

© Rachel Axten-Higgs 2014
First published in 2014 by
Hodder Education,
An Hachette UK Company
Carmelite House
50 Victoria Embankment
London EC4Y 0DZ

Impression number   10 9 8 7 6 5
Year   2019 2018 2017

Cover illustration by Sandy Lightley
Illustrations by Marleen Visser
Typeset in Swissforall in 15pt by Resolution
Printed in Italy

A catalogue record for this title is available from the British Library

ISBN: 978 1471 830266

Contents

Let's look at non-fiction

Why do bats hang upside down?

Bats are nocturnal. This means they are active at night and inactive during the day. At night they fly around and catch insects and small animals to eat. During the day they hang upside down in places (caves, under bridges or inside trees) that are quiet and unlikely to be disturbed.

There are two main reasons why bats hang upside down. Firstly, by hanging upside down, bats are able to hide themselves from animals and birds wishing to hunt them.

The other reason is that this is the best position for them to take-off from. By hanging upside down they can drop from the branch and take flight as they fall. They can do this quickly. They might have to escape in a hurry – even while they are sleeping!

Helpful hints

Explanation texts tell us how or why something happens, e.g. how a house is built. The key features of this type of text are:

- title – this should tell you what the writing is about or could be a question that the text is going to answer.
- opening statement – this should be general and briefly explain what the writing is about.
- paragraphs – the text should be in time order if it is about a process and be broken into smaller paragraphs. These should be linked for the reader.
- connectives – these should show time (then, next …) and reasons (because, so, therefore …)

I can answer questions about a text.

I can identify features of non-fiction texts.

I can understand how paragraphs can be used to organise a text.

Answering questions about a text

1 Read the text about bats on page 4 and then answer the following questions:
- a When do bats catch food to eat?
- b What foods do bats eat?
- c What is the best position for bats to take-off from?
- d Name two places where bats hang upside down.

2 Paragraphs group similar information together to make it easier for the reader to understand the text.

These paragraph headings are muddled up. Work out which heading fits with each paragraph. For example, paragraph 1 = introduction.
- a Paragraph 1 _____
- b Paragraph 2 _____
- c Paragraph 3 _____

Hiding   Introduction   Taking-off

3 The text about bats on page 4 is an 'explanation' text. Look at the list of key features below and select two that are from explanation texts:
- Numbered steps
- Time and causal connectives
- Headline
- Written in columns
- Paragraphs written in logical steps

Let me persuade you

Authors of adverts choose their words carefully to make products sound appealing. Adjectives are often used in adverts to emphasise positive aspects and make comparisons between other products, e.g. 'better' or 'extra' or 'special'.

Introducing the NEW...
and EXCITING...

WATERSCOPE

The newest item in our award-winning science range. The Waterscope's powerful magnifier enables you to explore the underwater world as never before. Make a day at the seaside one you will never forget with the fabulous Waterscope!

Can you afford to miss out on this exciting new invention?

This invention has made it so much easier to teach children about underwater habitats as they can see it for real, for themselves!
Teacher

Find out more at: www.waterscopes.com

Helpful hints

Persuasive writing is when a writer uses language to try and make a reader agree with their point of view. Adverts are persuasive texts as they try to persuade the reader to buy a new product. Key features of this type of text are:

- a bold heading to catch the reader's attention
- an introductory paragraph about the new product
- each paragraph states a reason/opinion to encourage the reader to think about the product
- the reader is asked questions to try to encourage them to think about whether they need the product or not
- a conclusion that supports the introductory paragraph. This could include quotes from users of the product
- photographs and other illustrations to catch the reader's attention

Glossary

magnifier
a device that makes an image or object appear bigger
habitat
the natural home or environment of an animal or plant
invention
a new device or process that is developed following experimentation

Engaging a reader

1 The advert on page 6 is a persuasive text. Adjectives (words which describe nouns) are used in adverts to help make the product seem more appealing to the reader. Re-read the advert and write five different adjectives that have been used to describe the product.

Talk Partners

Create your own advert. Think about an ordinary object you use regularly at home or school such as a plate or pencil case. Try to convince your partner it is a fantastic object they have to own. Jot down some adjectives which would make the object seem appealing. For example, *bright, pretty, better*... When you have finished, work with a partner and give each other feedback on how convincing the adverts were.

2 Different types of sentences are used in the advert on page 6:

- **questions** (*Can you afford to miss out on this exciting new invention?*)

- **exclamations** (*'This invention has made it so much easier to teach children about underwater habitats as they can see it for real, for themselves!'*)

- **statements** (*The newest item in our award-winning science range.*)

Each of these sentences has a different punctuation mark at the end. Using the advert, write one example of each type of sentence, with the correct punctuation at the end:

a a statement   b a question   c an exclamation

A report

What might you see in a desert?

On Earth, more than one-seventh of the land is desert. A desert is an area that has little rain throughout the year.

Most people think deserts are completely covered by sand but some are covered in pebbles and rocks – or even salt where lakes have dried up.

Special plants such as cacti have had to adapt to be able to grow in desert conditions. For example, they are able to store water in their thick stems. Other plants grow long roots so they are able to draw up water from deep underground.

Some animals, like coyotes, are able to live in the deserts by adapting to the surroundings. Many of these animals are nocturnal and able to burrow or hide under rocks.

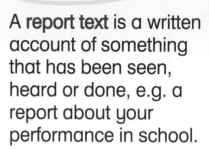

Helpful hints

A **report text** is a written account of something that has been seen, heard or done, e.g. a report about your performance in school.

Glossary

cacti
a plant with a thick stem which usually has spines rather than leaves
coyote
a wolf-like dog
nocturnal
active at night
desert
a dry region on Earth, usually sandy with little rainfall

I can identify the main points in a text.

I can listen carefully in discussion and make sensible comments.

Identifying main points

1 To show you have understood the main points of the text on page 8, write down three key pieces of information (in your own words). Remember, key pieces of information contain the main points of the piece of writing.

Talk Partners

Share your points with another learner. Do you both agree? If necessary, improve on your key points.

2 Common word endings are: -ing, -ed, -es. These are called suffixes. Draw the table below. Re-read the information on page 8 and write words with these suffixes from the text in each column. Then add 3 of your own words to each column. Make sure they fit the spelling pattern.

Words ending -ing	Words ending -ed	Words ending -es

Writing notes

1 Look back at the texts on pages 4 and 8 and make some short notes about nocturnal animals. Do this in steps:
- First, look for the word 'nocturnal' in the text to find the part of the text you need.
- Re-read these parts of the text. What key information do they give about nocturnal animals?

2 Choose another nocturnal animal from this list:
badger, hamster, leopard, skunk, mouse

Copy and complete this table. Using books or the internet, make brief notes of the key information based on the column heading.

What the animal eats	Where the animal lives	Predators of the animal

Writing presentation

1 Using your notes and the table below, plan three short paragraphs to write about your chosen animal.

Paragraph	What I will include in my paragraph
1 Introduce the animal and explain what nocturnal means.	
2 Give an explanation about what the animal eats and why it hunts at night.	
3 Give an explanation about where the animal lives, its predators and how it has adapted to its surroundings.	

2 Now write a short report about the animal. Afterwards, check through your work and underline any words that are spelt incorrectly. Write these words in your spelling journal and practise spelling them correctly.

A newspaper report

Helpful hints

Newspaper reports are written in the past tense as they are reporting something that has already happened. The first paragraph of a newspaper report gives an overview of:

- **who** was involved
- **what** happened
- **where** the event happened
- **when** it happened
- **why** it happened or why it is being written about now.

In the paragraphs that follow, more information is given about the story. There will be some facts and comments from other people who have been involved. However, you must leave out your own opinions.

Did you know?

Newspapers have been around for a very long time. The first English newspaper was printed in 1641. The first American newspaper was printed in 1690. The first Australian newspaper was published in 1803.

School Jumps for Joy!

Yesterday, children at Brookside School in England were celebrating their success at breaking a world record in skipping.

The children had been practising for months in their attempt to break the record for the largest number of children skipping using only one rope. The previous record had been set by children at Green Acre School in Australia and involved 156 children. Yesterday, 205 children at Brookside School skipped under one rope for 26 turns.

Headteacher Claire Axten said, "I am delighted the hard work of the staff and children involved in this project has been recognised on a national scale."

Engaging the reader

1 Look at the newspaper report on page 11. Make notes from the first paragraph using the following headings:

a **Who** is the report about?
b **What** have they done?
c **Where** did the event happen?
d **When** did the event happen?
e **Why** did the event happen?

2 The author of the newspaper report on page 11 has written an interesting first paragraph to gain the reader's attention. The other paragraphs also include features which will keep us engaged in reading. Copy the table below and write examples of each feature.

A comparison to show how amazing the record was	
A quote	
A fact	

3 a Use the headings below to make notes about an event. This should be something that you have been involved in, such as a school play, fundraising event, club meeting or competition.

Paragraph	What I will include in my paragraph
1 Details about what the event is, when and where it took place and who is involved.	
2 Information about how the event began and then built up. Include details about who, what and why.	
3 A quote from someone involved (this can be made up).	
4 How the event ended.	

b Now use your notes to write an interesting report that engages your reader.

Types of sentence

1 Write each of these sentences and identify whether they are:

- **a question** (asking you something)
- **a statement** (telling you something)
- **an order** (telling you to do something).

a How old are you?
b Cheetahs run very fast.
c Go and finish your homework.
d Help me finish this work.
e Where do you live?
f A table usually has four legs.

Now underline the verb in each sentence.

Helpful hints

Facts are pieces of information that are true and often given as statements. For example: *Apples can be red or green.*
Opinions are people's ideas or thoughts about something. For example: *Apples are delicious!*

Talk Partners

What do you notice about the position of the verb in questions, statements and orders?

2 For each of the statements below, write whether they are facts (F) or opinions (O):

a New Delhi is the capital city of India.
b Italian food is the tastiest food in the world.
c Sailfish are the world's fastest animals in water.
d The Pacific Ocean is the world's largest ocean.
e Hot weather is better than cold weather.
f The cheetah is the world's fastest land animal.
g Reading is boring.

13

I can re-read my writing to check it makes sense.

I can present a point of view in ordered points.

My opinion

Children should not be allowed to bring mobile phones to school.

Helpful hints

When presenting your point of view, first outline what your opinion is. In the next paragraph give reasons for your opinion. Then repeat your opinion with the most important reason why the reader should agree with it.

1 Answer the following questions about the statement above.
  a What opinion is being given in this statement?
  b Do you agree or disagree with the opinion?
  c What are the reasons for **your** opinion?
  d Write two headings for the statement above: FOR and AGAINST. Make notes under each heading.

Talk Partners

With a partner, compare your answers to the questions above. Add more information to the 'FOR' and 'AGAINST' columns, based on your discussion.

Writing presentation

Write about whether children should be allowed to bring mobile phones to school, using your notes from activity 1. Include the following paragraphs in your writing

Notes

  a **Introductory paragraph** – state your opinion.
  b **Middle paragraph** – give reasons for your opinion.
  c **Final paragraph** – restate your opinion with your most important reason.

Argument texts

Should children keep animals as pets?	
Arguments for	**Arguments against**
Children learn to be responsible.	Children are often too busy to look after a pet properly.
Children have to be reliable as the pet depends on them for food, warmth and love.	Adults end up having to look after the pet when the child gets bored of it.
Children have fun playing with the animal.	Some animals do not like being kept as pets.
	Children are not old enough to be responsible for another living thing.

1 Read the text above and decide which side of the argument you agree with. Make some notes about your argument by thinking about the opposite view. For example, 'children have fun playing with the animal' versus 'some animals carry harmful diseases which can be passed onto them when handling the animal'. Try to use some connectives in your notes.

Glossary

responsible: to think of others and have a job to do
reliable: able to be trusted
depend: relies on
verbal: using spoken words

Helpful hints

Argument texts show both sides of the argument so that the reader can consider the different opinions and make a choice. Key features of balanced arguments:
- a title – a simple statement or question that shows the issue being argued
- a short opening to explain the argument
- points in favour of the argument – facts and evidence to support these
- points against the argument – facts and evidence to support these
- connectives are used to structure the argument
- a conclusion – each side of the argument is summarised and then your own view given.

Argument texts can also simply give one side of the argument.

Debates are spoken 'verbal arguments' where both sides get to state their case. A vote is then held to decide which argument was the most convincing.

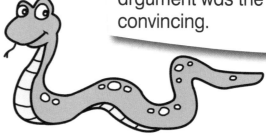

I understand how points are ordered to make a coherent argument.

I can respond to main ideas with relevant suggestions and comments.

Debate

1 Re-write these points of an argument in order so that they make sense. The connectives are shown in bold.

- **Finally**, I believe that children will learn to be responsible through keeping a pet. **For instance**, they have to put the pet before themselves.
- **Secondly**, pets can become a good friend to children **in that** some enjoy being handled and spoken to.
- I think that children should be allowed to keep animals as pets.
- **Firstly**, I believe children should learn to be reliable. **After all**, caring for a pet requires them to do this.
- **Also**, pets are fun. **For example**, children could build tunnels for hamsters to run through.

2 Use the structure below to help you make notes about why children should **not** be allowed pets.

a   State your viewpoint. *(I think that children should not be allowed to keep animals as pets.)*

b   Give your most important argument first. *(Firstly, ...)*

c   Give another argument with extra details to back it up. *(Secondly, ...)*

d   Give another argument with extra details to back it up. *(Thirdly, ...)*

e   Give your final argument. This could be the one that you think is the most convincing. For example, some animals do not like being kept as pets. *(Finally, ...)*

Talk Partners

Find a partner who has the opposite point of view to you. Using the notes:

- state your viewpoint and say why you think as you do.
- your partner then states their viewpoint and explains why they think as they do.

Layout and presentation of arguments

1 You are going to write an argument either for or against:
Should children keep animals as pets?
Start by making notes about what you will include in each paragraph using the following headings:

- **Introduction:** What the question is and what your viewpoint is. E.g. *I believe that children should not be allowed to keep animals as pets.*

- **Paragraph 2:** Your first argument with details to back it up. E.g. *Firstly, I think this because children are not old enough to care for them properly. Children enjoy buying the animal, but then grow bored of having to feed and clean up after it everyday. They would rather be playing with their friends!*

- **Paragraph 3:** Put forward another point that supports your argument. Remember to use examples to back it up. E.g. *My second point is …*

- **Paragraph 4:** Finish with the final point of your argument. Since this is the last one read by the reader, it should play on their emotions. E.g. *My final point is that the animals do not like being kept as pets. They would rather be left alone than played with like a toy.*

Now use the notes to write your argument. Keep your handwriting clear and evenly sized. Afterwards, check through your work and underline any words that are spelt incorrectly. Write these words in your spelling journal and practise spelling them correctly.

Try this

Connectives are words or phrases that link parts of sentences together. For example, however, but, then, yet, as. Look through your writing and identify the connectives you have used. Change or add to these, so that you have connectives that help you structure the argument.

Arguments

I believe that children should, if they want to, be allowed to stay in the school building during lunchtimes and breaktimes.

Firstly, children are often bored during free time as there is nothing for them to do. This can lead to arguments between friends. This disrupts the children's learning as they are upset when they come back to school. If they were able to stay in the classroom they could do activities such as extra learning, play games or read books. These activities could be very positive for children's education.

Secondly, children are sometimes too tired to run around outside. They may have had a bad night's sleep or feel unwell. If they are made to go outside then they may run out of energy before the next lesson and not concentrate very well in school. This would not happen if they stayed in and rested during breaktime.

Finally, children would be able to have their snacks and drinks seated at a table rather than running around the playground. Drinks can be spilt outside as children run into one another. They could also choke on their food when they are running.

Talk Partners

Do you agree with this argument? Discuss your viewpoint with a partner. Can you think of other reasons why children should or should not be allowed to stay in during free time? Make a list with your partner.

Arguments

1 The following are counter-arguments (the opposite viewpoint) for the argument text on page 18. Write them in the correct order.

a Children engage in lots of learning seated at desks during the school day.

b There are many activities for children to do outside.

c The classroom would become untidy if children were allowed to eat and drink in it.

d I believe that children should not be allowed to stay in during breaktimes.

e Children learn to manage friendships by resolving problems.

f Children don't have to run around outside. They could sit and relax on a bench instead.

2 Here are some additional arguments against children being allowed to stay in during breaktime.
Write a counter-argument for each one.

a Children would have to be supervised in the classroom.

b Exercise is good for children.

c Children would get bored being in the same room all day.

I can re-read my writing to check my punctuation and grammar.

I can summarise a sentence or a paragraph in a limited number of words.

Summarising a paragraph

1 Look back at your writing from page 17 and summarise what it is about. Use the information in the Helpful hints box to help you work through the process. The summary should be no more than 20 words for each paragraph.

2 Write a paragraph about yourself, where you live, your family and what your interests are in no more than 100 words.

3 Re-write the paragraph from activity 2 in only 50 words. Make sure you have all the main points.

4 Re-write your summary from activity 3 using only 25 words. You may have to take out:
- articles (*e.g. a, an, the*)
- prepositions *(words usually preceding nouns showing a relationship to another word, such as after, on, for)*

Helpful hints

Summarising is identifying the key points from a longer piece of writing so that it becomes a shorter piece of writing.

To summarise you need to:
- **skim the text** and find answers related to questions such as **why, what, when, where, who** and **how**
- **identify the main point of the text.** For example: What is the purpose of the text? What have you learned that you did not know before?
- **identify the main point of each paragraph.** What is the paragraph about?
- use the main points to **write your summary.**

Different types of non-fiction

1 Match the following texts to their key features:

    a   explanation texts contain   b   report texts contain

    c   newspaper reports contain   d   argument texts contain

1	2	3	4
Headline First paragraph summarising key information Written in columns	Time and causal connectives Opening statement Time-ordered paragraphs	Introduction stating argument Ordered reasons with evidence Summary of main argument	General opening statement Technical vocabulary related to subject Concluding statement Diagrams to explain part of the text

2 Which text types are these sentences from?

    a   Can you afford to miss out on our amazing new product?

    b   Bob Hind is celebrating his gold medal in the 100m sprint today.

    c   Cheetahs are the world's fastest animals, reaching speeds of 68 mph.

    d   Some people believe that children should start school at the age of 3.

What have I learnt?

There are many types of non-fiction texts. Can you:
* name some different types of non-fiction texts?
* say the key features of some non-fiction texts?
* state a point of view (an opinion) about a piece of writing?
* remember how to summarise longer passages into shorter ones?

Unit 2 How are stories put together?

Story openings

A

The Happy Alien

Last summer, a very strange thing happened to my gran. She woke up to find a bus ticket on her table. This may not sound very strange to you, but trust me! It was strange.

The Happy Alien by Jean Ure featured in *The Story Shop* by Nikki Gamble

C

Escape from Pompeii

On a hillside overlooking the sparkling bay of Naples, the Roman city of Pompeii glimmered in the sunlight.

Escape from Pompeii by Christina Balit

B

The Leopard

I first saw the leopard when I was crossing the small stream at the bottom of the hill.
The ravine was so deep that for most of the day it remained in shadow. This encouraged many birds and animals to emerge from cover during daylight hours. Few people ever passed that way: only milkmen and charcoal-burners from the surrounding villages.

The Leopard by Ruskin Bond featured in *The Story Shop* by Nikki Gamble

D

Why The Whales Came

"You keep away from the birdman, Gracie," my father had warned me often enough. "Keep well clear of him, you hear me now?" And we never would have gone anywhere near him, Daniel and I, had the swans not driven us away from the pool under Gweal Hill where we always went to sail our boats.

Why the Whales Came by Michael Morpurgo

I can explore different openings to stories.

Adding detail to stories

1 Read the story openings on page 22. Write down what type of opening each one is. Use the Helpful hints box opposite.

2 Look at some story openings in books. Identify the type of opening for each.

3 Choose one story opening you particularly like. Copy it out. Write three reasons why you find it an interesting and engaging opening.

Helpful hints

Authors plan the openings of stories carefully to make the reader interested and excited so that they read the rest of the story. There are different types of story openings:

* action – *something happens straight away*
* dialogue – *characters speak to one another*
* setting focus – *the setting is described in detail*
* character focus – *a character or characters are introduced to the reader straight away*
* narrative hook – *something is suggested to the reader to make them curious.*

Glossary

dialogue: a conversation between two or more people that is written down

character: a person who is in a story, play or film

setting: the place where an event or action takes place

Story outcomes

1 Look at the following story opening:

> Long ago in the land of Persia, there lived a poor woodcutter called Ali Baba. One day, while he was working in the middle of the forest, he saw some horsemen coming his way. They were shouting and making a loud noise, and poor Ali Baba knew at once that they were a band of robbers. As quickly as he could, he climbed up the nearest tree, and hid among the branches.

This is the beginning of a well-known story using traditional story language.

Write the beginning of the same story but with three different types of openings:

a dialogue
b a description of setting
c a character description of Ali Baba.

Helpful hints

Look back to the Helpful hints box on page 23 to remind yourself of the different types of story openings.

2 Read the story opening in activity 1 again. Underline any words that have double consonants. For example, mi**dd**le, begi**nn**ing, ha**pp**en.

Talk Partners

Read one of your story openings from activity 1 to a partner. Can he/she guess which type of opening it is? Take turns to read different examples to each other.

I can identify and understand the main stages in a story.

I can identify the key events in stories.

Story planning

Planning for a story can be done in five stages. Look at the story plan below. It is in the shape of a hill to show that events lead up to the climax/conflict and then are resolved at the end.

Helpful hints

There are five main stages to all stories:
- **the beginning** (this introduces the story)
- **build up** (these are the events that will lead to a problem)
- **climax/conflict** (this is the problem that needs solving)
- **resolution** (these are the events leading to the ending)
- **the end** (the problem is resolved and the story ends).

Story Planning Hill

3. Climax/conflict

The hare is tired and hot so sits down to rest as he knows the tortoise is a long way behind. Hare falls asleep.

2. Build up

The day of the race – a hot day. Hare sprints off ahead. Tortoise is left behind, going very slowly.

4. Resolution

Tortoise passes the hare while he is asleep. Hare wakes up and sprints off, but the tortoise is already crossing the finishing line.

1. Beginning

The hare boasts that he is the fastest animal in the forest. The tortoise agrees to a race.

5. End

Animals cheer the tortoise. The hare is embarrassed and never boasts again.

Writing a story from a plan

1
a What title would you give to the story on page 25?
b What is the climax of the story?
c What important lesson does the hare learn?
d What genre of story is it? Use the information about genres to explain your answer.

Writing presentation

Use the plan on page 25 to write the story in full. Add extra detail to create 5 paragraphs (one for each box shown on the plan) showing each of the main stages of the story. You could add details about the setting and characters, and dialogue, to make it exciting for your reader.

Afterwards, check through your work and underline any words that are spelt incorrectly. Write these words in your spelling journal and practise spelling them correctly.

Try this

Write two different endings to your story. In the first one, the hare wins the race. In the second, both animals cross the line at the same time.

Did you know?

There are many different genres (types) of fiction to read and enjoy. Which of these genres would you like to read?

Fantasy – these often take place in imaginary worlds.
Fable – short stories that usually include animals as the characters and have a moral.
Mystery – these often have a detective who has to solve a crime.
Adventure – these focus on an adventure where there is risk or danger.
Science Fiction – these include imaginative and futuristic settings, often including time or space travel.
Historical – these focus on events in the past.

Story stages

1 All stories have five key parts to them. Choose a story you know well and create a story plan for it, like the example on page 25. Add notes to your plan to clearly show each part of the story:

1. Beginning
2. Build up
3. Climax/conflict
4. Resolution
5. Ending

2 Use your plan to draw a picture for each stage to remind you of the key details of the story.

Beginning – The Gingerbread Man

Talk Partners

Use your plan to tell the story to a partner.

Think carefully about the expression that you use to help keep your partner interested. Expression means making the words more exciting by using different voices for the characters and narrative. For example, a scary voice for a bad character and a sweet voice for a young character.

I can investigate the past, present and future tenses of verbs.

Tenses

1 This table shows you the past, present and future versions of two verbs used regularly:

Past	Present	Future
to be		
I **was** he/she/it **was** we/you/they **were**	I **am** he/she/it **is** we/you **are**	I **will be** he/she/it **will be** we/you **will be**
to have		
I **had** he/she/it **had** we/you **had**	I **have** he/she/it **has** we/you **have**	I **will have** he/she/it **will have** we/you **will have**

Write each of these sentences, choosing the correct version of the verb 'to be' or 'to have' to complete the sentence. Write next to the sentence whether it is in the past, present or future tense.

a I _____ three cats.

b I _____ happy when I won the prize.

c You _____ welcome to come to my house.

d She _____ neat handwriting.

e It _____ raining outside today.

f We _____ lots of balloons at your next party.

g She _____ older than me.

h It _____ been raining for two months before this sunshine came.

i You _____ a good job if you work hard at school.

j They _____ happy to see me yesterday.

Helpful hints

The tense of a verb shows whether the action has happened:
- in the past tense.
  E.g. *I played football.*
- in the present tense.
  E.g. *I am playing football.*
- in the future tense.
  E.g. *I will play football.*

Tenses are helpful in writing as they signal to the reader about the timing of events in the story.

Key points in stories

Escape from Pompeii

EXTRACT A:
When Tranio and Livia woke and looked out, they were horrified. Pompeii was getting further and further away. The sky was now thick with pumice and black with ash … And then, in one terrible endless moment, they heard mighty Mount Versuvius roar.

EXTRACT B:
They had left just in time. Soon the sea sank back from the shore and even the fishes were stranded there.

EXTRACT C:
Then something happened … The stone steps creaked, the flaps began to rattle and the buildings quivered.

EXTRACT D:
No one noticed two small children climb up the narrow plank of a small Greek cargo ship and hide beneath a pile of coloured rugs. Dusty and tired in their hiding-place they soon fell asleep. But as they slept the anxious captain untied his boat. He sensed the winds had changed direction and that the air was uncomfortably hot.

EXTRACT E:
From his window, young Tranio listened to the noise humming from bars, taverns and shops around him, and to the busy tradesmen haggling in the streets below.

All extracts from: Escape from Pompeii by Christina Balit

I can identify adverbs and their impact on meaning.

Ordering events

1 Write the letters (A, B, C...) from the extracts on page 29 to show the correct order of the story. What you know about the five stages of stories should help you with this!

2 Write these sentences, adding an adverb to each:
- a The boy looked _____ at his teacher.
- b My cousin visited _____ .
- c We _____ grabbed the apples from the tree.
- d Raj was _____ humming to himself.
- e The children waited _____ outside the office.

3 Rewrite Extract C by adding an adverb to each of these verbs: *creaked*, *rattle* and *quivered*. For example, *The stone steps creaked **quietly**. Quietly* is the adverb as it describes the verb in more detail.

Helpful hints

Adverbs give extra information about a verb, adjective or another adverb by telling the reader **how**, **where** or **when** something happened.

- He ran **quickly** to the boat – quickly is an adverb that explains **how** he ran to the boat.
- We have to leave **soon** – soon is an adverb that explains **when** something happened.
- We attend school **here** – here is an adverb that shows **where** something happens.

Other examples of adverbs are: **always**, **gladly**, **happily**, **yesterday** …

Ending stories

1 Read these story endings.
Find and copy an example of the punctuation marks listed in the Helpful hints box opposite.
For example:
Full stop = *Mum says that's OK.*

Helpful hints

When reading, look carefully at the punctuation marks as they help you to understand the text:
- **full stops** make you stop
- **commas** make you pause
- **exclamation marks** signal excitement or surprise
- **question marks** signal a question
- **speech marks** show the words a character speaks.

The Happy Alien

Ria says what's happened is that Her Next Door has turned Gran into a fellow alien, but Mum says that's OK.

'So long as she's a *happy* alien, that's all that matters!'

The Happy Alien by Jean Ure featured in The Story Shop by Nikki Gamble

The Leopard

'Yes,' I said. 'He was a beautiful leopard.'

I walked home through the silent forest. It was very silent, almost as though the birds and animals knew that their trust had been **violated**.

The Leopard by Ruskin Bond featured in The Story Shop by Nikki Gamble

Why the Whales Came

Everyone drank from the well of Samson that day as if it were the **elixir** of life, and after that no one ever doubted the Birdman's story, not in my hearing anyway.

Why the Whales Came by Michael Morpurgo

Glossary

elixir:
a potion
violated:
broken a rule or treated with disrespect

I can retell events from the text in response to questions.

I can explore different endings to stories.

Story endings

1 In the story 'The Leopard', the leopard is no longer alive at the end of the story.

    a How do you know this from the words used at the ending of the story?

    b Why was the forest 'silent' at the end of the story?

    c What trust do you think had been broken between men and animals?

2 At the beginning of the story in extract D on page 22, Gracie is told not to go near the Birdman. Now that you have read the ending of the story on page 31, answer these questions.

    a Do you think she obeyed this instruction? Explain your answer.

    b Was the water in the well of Samson good or bad? Explain your answer.

    c Did people believe the Birdman's story? How do you know?

Helpful hints

Remember the different story genres:
- Fantasy
- Mystery
- Adventure
- Science Fiction
- Historical

Look back at page 26 if you need a reminder about these genres.

3 What genre does the story 'The Happy Alien' come from? Support your answer with evidence from extracts on pages 22 and 31.

Creating a story plan

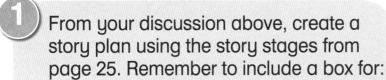
Talk Partners

In a group of 3 or 4, choose a beginning and ending that belongs to the same story. Discuss the following:

a What events might happen because of the beginning?

b What might have led to the ending?

c Questions you could ask to find out more about events in the story.

1 From your discussion above, create a story plan using the story stages from page 25. Remember to include a box for:

a a beginning

b the build up – events that cause the problem

c the climax of the story – this is the problem that needs solving

d the resolution leading to the ending – how does the climax resolve itself?

e the ending – everything is resolved and the story ends.

2 Use your plan to write the story by adding details to each of the boxes. Write each stage of the story in a separate paragraph. Afterwards, check through your story and underline any words that are spelt incorrectly. Write these words in your spelling journal and practise spelling them correctly.

What have I learnt?

Read your story. Check that it contains the following:

• a clear beginning

• a clear ending

• five clear stages (beginning, build-up, climax, events leading to ending, ending)

• vocabulary which is precise and engages the reader

• the correct punctuation marks, for example, speech marks.

I can use paragraphs to help me organise my writing.

Editing a story

1 Look at the 'What have I learnt?' clipboard on page 33. Read through the story you have written and check you have met each of the criteria. Think about:

- use of vocabulary – are the descriptions both clear and engaging?
- correct punctuation marks – do sentences end with the correct punctuation? Do sentences start with capital letters? Are there clear paragraph breaks?

Make changes in a different colour pen to show you have edited your work.

Read your story to a partner.
Ask for feedback on:

- their enjoyment of the story
- whether the beginning, middle and end link and build up well
- any parts they think you could improve, e.g. description of the setting or a particular character – or more details on one of the events.

2 Think about the feedback given by your partner and decide whether any changes need to be made. You do not have to agree with your partner, but it's possible their suggestions would make your writing even better! Make the changes to your story in a different colour pen.

Mixed-up stories

a Little Red Riding Hood swapped a cow for some beans, and crossed the bridge that a troll lived under.

b Jack put on a bright red cape, and fell asleep in Baby Bear's bed.

c The three billy goats gruff broke into the three bears' cottage, and was pounced on by a wolf disguised as granny.

d Goldilocks saw the fresh green grass and climbed a huge beanstalk.

1 Read the sentences from the well-known stories above. They are all mixed up! Re-write each sentence so that the characters and settings make sense again.

Tenses

2 Choose one of the stories from page 35 and write a story plan for it. Include the following sections in your plan:
- opening
- build up
- climax/conflict
- resolution
- ending.

3 Complete the following sentences in the future tense using either **will** or **am/is are + going to.**

a John Smith is _____ be the next president. (a prediction)

b They _____ call you later. (a promise)

c Sephina _____ help me move this heavy table. (an action)

d Kyros is _____ to invite me to his party. (a plan)

Talk Partners Jumble the story summaries on page 35 in a different way, *e.g. The three billy goats gruff put on a bright red cape, and fell asleep in Baby Bear's bed.* Choose one you think is funny, and tell your partner the story. You could add some details to make the story even funnier.

Helpful hints

The simple **future tense** is used to show that something will take place in the future. There are two ways to write a sentence in the simple future tense:

Using **will + verb**
I **will help** him later.
The sun **will rise** tomorrow.
They **will go** to the park on Wednesday.

Using **am/is/are + going to + verb**
I **am going to meet** Ishaq tonight.
She **is going to make** Chelsea a cake.
They **are going to meet** this afternoon.

Rules for the future tense:

will + verb to show a future action, promise or prediction
- I **will call** you when I arrive. (an action)
- I **will vote** for you. (a promise)
- Zara Naim **will win** the race. (a prediction)

am/is/are + going to + verb to show a plan, or can also be used to show a prediction
- They **are going to drive** all the way to Cairo. (a plan)
- Zara Naim **is going to win** the race. (a prediction)

Improving my writing

1 Use the table below to help you rewrite these sentences so they are more effective. Write each sentence, replace the verb and decide which adjective and adverb to add.

a The man walked to the shop to buy a present.

b The girl played on the swing in the park.

c The tiger hid in the bushes before jumping to catch his prey.

d I walked in the golden field of corn.

e He ran onto the sand and shouted at the top of his voice.

replacement verbs	adjectives	adverbs
strode	angry	happily
walked	happy	gloomily
skipped	rusty	quietly
scampered	squeaky	joyfully
disappeared	quiet	grumpily
meet	best	
screamed	golden	
bellowed	cold	
yelled	loud	

Helpful hints

Adjectives and adverbs turn writing into a visual picture. Remember, an **adverb** is a word that can be added to a verb or adjective to give extra information about how, where or when something happened. A **verb** is a word used to describe an action. **Adjectives** are describing words.

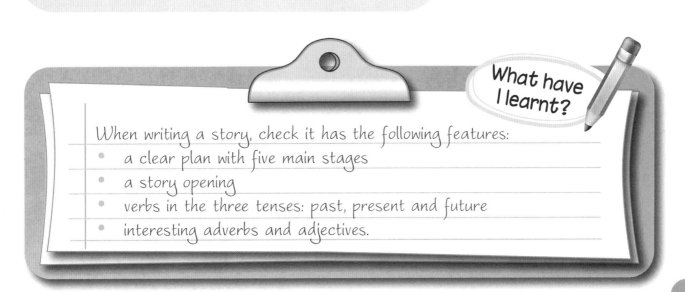

What have I learnt?

When writing a story, check it has the following features:
* a clear plan with five main stages
* a story opening
* verbs in the three tenses: past, present and future
* interesting adverbs and adjectives.

Unit 3 Looking at poetry

Limerick fun

What a fearless magician is Spring –
you really can't teach her a thing!
In she sneaks on a **breeze**,
draws the leaves from their trees …
just when Winter thought *he* was still King!

By Judith Nicholls

Glossary

breeze:
a gentle wind

There once was a man from Peru
Who dreamt that he swallowed his shoe
He woke up in fright
In the mid of the night
To learn that his dream had come true!

Anonymous

Expressing meaning

1 Read the limericks on page 38 in your head. What do you notice about the rhyming pattern? Is the pattern the same in both limericks? Write down the pairs of rhyming words used in each limerick. Add three other rhyming words to each pair, e.g. *Spring and thing (bring, sting, swing).*

2 Practise reading the limericks aloud. As you read, emphasise the rhymes at the end of each line so that they can be heard clearly.

3 Practise reading a limerick aloud as if you were cross. Think about the tone you will use. Read the limerick again as if you were happy. What is the difference in tone?

Helpful hints

When reading aloud to an audience, you need to think carefully about the tone of your voice. Tone means the pitch and volume of your voice. For example, soft, soothing sounds when saying words would indicate happiness or pleasure. Harsh, loud delivery of words would show anger. Punctuation marks can give clues about tone:

- **!** an exclamation mark means your voice needs to indicate emotion. This could be excitement, happiness or surprise
- **?** a question mark means you should raise your voice at the end of the sentence
- often CAPITALS mean you need to raise the volume of your voice.

Talk Partners Read a limerick aloud to a partner and ask them for feedback. Did you look at your partner while reading it? Was your voice loud enough? Did they hear the rhymes clearly and understand that the poem was funny?

Haikus

Outbreak of Peace, Haiku

My mum declares peace.
She hands out bouquets of smiles.
Laughter like church bells.

By Pie Corbett

The Haiku Monster

The Haiku monster
Gobbles up the syllables
Crunching words and CHOMP!

By Paul Cookson

Haiku

Learn to write haiku
The number of syllables
Totals seventeen

By Rachel Axten-Higgs

Did you know?

Haikus are Japanese poems that have seventeen syllables. A syllable is a unit of pronunciation that includes one vowel phoneme. For example, *hap/py* has two syllables. Haikus have three lines with five syllables in the first line, seven in the second line and five in the last line. Originally they were written to give images of the natural world, but now include a wider range of topics. Born in 1644, Matsuo Kinsaku wrote the first ever haiku. So it could be said that he invented this form of poetry.

Meanings in poetry

1 In the first haiku on page 40, the line 'laughter like church bells' is a form of imagery. It compares the laughter to the sound of church bells chiming. This is to show that the laughter is continuous and rhythmic like bells. This is a simile, as it compares one thing to another. Rewrite this line to compare the laughter to something else. Remember the line needs to be five syllables, so think carefully about which words to use!

2 Look at line two of the Haiku Monster on page 40. Draw a picture of the image from this line. What does the monster look like? How does the poem help you remember the format of a haiku?

3 How does the final poem, Haiku, on page 40 help you to remember what a haiku is? Think about:
- How many syllables are needed for a haiku?
- How many syllables are needed per line?

Helpful hints

Imagery is when the writer creates a picture in the reader's head through using descriptive or **figurative language**. Often images are used that appeal to the reader's senses – look, sound, smell, taste. **Similes** are a form of figurative language as they compare one object to another to add description. They will always use 'as' or 'like' to introduce the image. For example:
- *The air was as cold as ice.*
- *The food felt like rough cloth in her mouth.*

Try this

Write a haiku. Make sure you have the correct number of syllables for each line. Choose a feature of nature to write about – just like the traditional haikus. For example, *trees, wind, flowers, birds.* Remember:
- Line 1 needs 5 syllables
- Line 2 needs 7 syllables
- Line 3 needs 5 syllables

Creating the mood

Helpful hints ⭐

- **Explicit** meanings are those clearly expressed by the author. For example: *There is a storm outside.*
- **Implicit** meanings are those that are implied (suggested) by the author, but not actually written. For example: *They stepped into the dark wood, the rain poured down and a cold wind whipped through the trees.* The implied meaning here is that something frightening might happen. This is not said, but can be inferred from your knowledge of settings such as this.
- **Powerful verbs** are verbs that give more detail about the action than ordinary verbs. For example: *whispered* instead of *said,* or, *stomped* instead of *walked.*

It's only the Storm

'What's that creature that rattles the roof?' implicit meaning
'Hush, it's only the storm.'

'What's blowing the tiles and branches off?'
'Hush, it's only the storm.' explicit meaning

'What's riding the sky like a wild white horse,
Flashing its teeth and stamping its hooves?' powerful verbs

'Hush, my dear, it's only the storm,
Racing the darkness till it catches the dawn.
Hush, my dear, it's only the storm.
When you wake in the morning, it will be gone.'

By David Greygoose

I can identify explicit and implicit meanings in texts.

I can use powerful verbs.

I can understand how descriptive language helps to create the mood.

Using verbs

1 On page 42, the poet tells us that there is a storm (explicit). However, he also implies there is thunder and lightning (implicit).

a Write down the lines of the poem that suggest the thunder and lightning.

b Write down the line of the poem that suggests the house is falling apart.

c Write down one explicit quotation from the poem.

2 The use of language in the poem on page 42 creates a picture for the reader, and sets the mood on how the poem should be read aloud.

a Write about how the poem makes you feel. Give details about the words or lines that make you feel that way. For example, *The poem makes me feel scared because the line that says, 'Flashing its teeth and stamping its hooves', tells me that the storm is very loud.' I can remember a storm like that, and it made me very frightened.*

3 Powerful verbs are used in this poem to create a clear picture for the reader. For example, the poet uses the verb 'rattles' (instead of 'shakes') as this gives the reader a clearer picture of what the rain on the roof sounds like. Find and write down two other powerful verbs the poet has used.

Poetry about a lifecycle

Angus Miller

Caterpillar
Occupation
Mastication
Everyday
Without a miss
Eating leaves
Till I am
A **chrysalis**
Which is a worm
That weaves
I'll sleep and spin
A thread of silk
Then one day
By and by
I'll get awake
And then I'll be
A gorgeous butterfly.

By Pamela Mordecai

Glossary

chrysalis:
a cocoon
occupation:
a job or profession
mastication:
the process by
which food is
crushed and
ground by teeth

I can identify explicit and implicit meaning in poems.

Meaning in poetry

1 The poem on page 44 details the lifecycle of a butterfly.
  a What does the poet mean by 'Occupation Mastication'?
  b Find and copy the lines that describe what a chrysalis is.
  c What is happening inside the chrysalis? Find and copy the lines.
  d Why has the poet used the name Angus Miller for the caterpillar at the start?

2 Find and copy the pairs of rhyming words in the poem on page 44.

3 Draw pictures to show each stage of the caterpillar's life as it turns into a butterfly. Put these in a circle to show a cycle. Add arrows between each stage: *caterpillar →
creating a chrysalis → turning into a butterfly →
egg laid to turn into a new caterpillar.*

Try this

Think about the lifecycle of a frog:
frogspawn → tadpole → frog
Write your own poem about this lifecycle using the structure from the poem on page 44. Include a simile. Use adjectives and adverbs to describe the frogspawn, e.g. *the frogspawn is bubbly and looks slimy,* and the movement of the tadpole, e.g. *the tadpole darts around the water quickly and in short bursts.*

Funny poems

The Sprat and the Jackfish

"Who cares if it's fair?"
the Jackfish said,
flicking its fin,
flashing its head.

"It's nothing to me
that you saw it first;
it's mine to keep
though you cry till you burst."

The small sprat flapped
its silver tail
and thought, "I wish
I were a whale.

I'd swallow this jackfish
with one gulp;
its body I would
turn to pulp.

Because you're that much
bigger than me,
you think you're the ruler
of the sea!

Well, take my worm
it's yours all right –
in this unfair world
it's might that's right."

"It's a juicy worm!"
the jackfish said,
flicking its fin,
flashing its head.

Then choking and twisting,
tormented it sped
along an invisible
line overhead ...

But the sprat did not see
as it went on its way.
"It's an unfair world,"
was all it could say.

By Grace Walker Gordon

Glossary

sprat:
a small type of fish

jackfish:
a type of fish found in
temperate and
tropical oceans

Reading aloud

1 Read the poem on page 46 in your head. Choose one of the verses and explain why you like it.

Talk Partners

With a partner, practise reading the poem aloud. Make sure you use the punctuation to help you read it with expression. Think about the volume and tone of your voice so that you show the different characters in the poem. Listen to feedback about your expression. Do the same for your partner.

Helpful hints

The way in which something is read impacts on how it is understood. A poem read in a bored, monotone voice, will not seem interesting to a listener. Punctuation marks may help you read a poem in a more expressive way:

- speech marks – show a character is speaking. Adapt your voice when you say these lines.
- ellipsis – shows a change in time. Pause and then change your voice for the next part. Make it louder or use a different tone.
- exclamation marks – used at the end of a humorous line. Read more lines in a fun way, drawing attention to the humorous rhyme.
- question marks – raise your voice at the end of the sentence.

What have I learnt?

When you read poetry, check that you can:
- understand the difference between reading silently and reading aloud.
- understand how meaning is expressed through use of voice and tone.
- spot how language is used to create mood and pictures for the reader.
- identify implicit meaning in poems.
- identify explicit meanings in poems.

Fiction

Read the extract and answer the questions which follow.

Maisie and Eddie hurried back along Albion Street. The professor had sent her out to buy two-pennyworth of nails to fasten up the last of the packing cases, which was good as he'd probably give Maisie a penny for herself. She'd be able to buy Eddie a nice bone at the butcher's.

"Oh, look, Eddie," Maisie muttered.

"Another nosey parker waiting outside. It's that newspaper article. It made it sound like the professor was keeping half the treasures of the Americas in our house. People think they're going to see great big gold statues, I suppose."

The man standing outside number 31 was quite elderly and was swathed in layers of scarves against the chilly March weather. His bowler hat was tipped forward over his nose, so that all Maisie could really see of him was a long, droopy moustache.

"I hope Gran hasn't noticed," Maisie told Eddie. "She hates all these people standing about. Maybe I can get rid of him." She coughed politely as she came up beside him. "May I help you, sir? I live here."

"Oh..." The man stared at her, and then took a step backwards, his head turning from side to side, like a trapped animal. Then he turned and hurried off down the street.

The Case of the Feathered Mask by Holly Webb

1   What were the 'two-pennyworth of nails' for? Choose one answer.
    a   to put up a picture
    b   to fasten up packing cases
    c   to mend a box
    d   to feed to a dog   (1)

2   What or who do you think Eddie is?   (1)

3   Find and write the sentence that explains why people were
    watching the house.   (1)

4   Find and write a sentence Maisie says to Eddie.   (1)

5   Find the description '*his head turning from side to side, like
    a trapped animal*'. Why does the author compare the man
    to a trapped animal?   (1)

6   Find and write three adjectives that describe the man.   (3)

7   Find and write the sentence that shows Maisie does not
    want her Gran to see the man outside.   (1)

8   How does the author show that Maisie tried to get the man's
    attention? Choose one answer.   (1)
    a   She called his name
    b   She coughed
    c   She waved at him
    d   She shook his arm

9   What does the author want us to think about the man
    outside the house? Choose one answer.
    a   He is someone Maisie knows
    b   He is unfriendly and nervous about being there
    c   He is a newspaper reporter
    d   He is a friend of the professor   (1)

10 Write two paragraphs for the next part of the story to show
    what happens next.   (5)
    You will need to decide:
    •   what the man wants from the professor
    •   what the man will try and do
    •   what was being put in the packing boxes and why.
    You will need to think about:
    •   the order of events in the paragraphs
    •   the language you will use, e.g. how to show a character is speaking.

PRACTICE TEST 1

Non-fiction

How Hot Air Balloons Work

Have you ever wondered how hot air balloons work? Read on to find out more about these fascinating flying contraptions!

The first fact that you need to know in order to understand how a hot air balloon works is that hot air always rises. This simple fact is the key to everything.

A hot-air balloon has three main parts to it: a canopy (called an envelope), made of thin silk; a basket, usually made of wicker; a burner, which is used to heat the air.

hot air rises

The envelope is laid out on the ground flat, and the basket and burners are attached. Then the burners are turned on. They use a gas called propane. This creates a large flame which heats up air. This hot air rises up inside the envelope and eventually fills it. As it fills up, the envelope rises up too, so it is sitting above the basket.

Once the envelope has been filled with hot air, the basket will begin to lift off the ground. The burners are kept on until the balloon has taken off and is flying high in the sky.

Of course, hot air will not stay hot forever, and the higher up you go from the ground, the colder it gets. This cold air cools the hot air trapped inside the envelope, so to keep the balloon up the pilot must turn on the burners occasionally. There is no way to steer a hot air balloon. The pilot simply drifts in the wind, keeping the balloon up for as long as possible, while looking for a safe place to land!

Read the text about hot air balloons and answer
the questions below.

1   What fact do you need to know to understand
    how a hot air balloon works? Choose the correct
    answer from this list.   (1)
    a   Balloons are hot
    b   Hot air rises
    c   The basket is made from wood
    d   Hot air falls

2   What does the pilot need to do to keep the balloon up in the air?   (1)

3   Name three parts of the balloon.   (3)

4   How does the pilot steer the balloon?   (1)

5   Which of these text types is the best description of the text?
    Write down two answers from the list below.   (2)
    •   Fiction
    •   Non-fiction
    •   Newspaper report
    •   Instructions
    •   Report
    •   Explanation
    •   Advert

6   Find and write an example of alliteration used in the text.   (1)

7   Who do you think this text is written for? Choose one answer
    from the list below.   (1)
    •   People who fly hot air balloons
    •   People who know about hot air balloons
    •   People who want to find out about hot air balloons

8   Read these sentences. Each one summarises a paragraph.
    Write them in the order in which they occur in the text.   (6)
    •   What a balloon consists of
    •   Introductory question to the reader
    •   Inflating the envelope
    •   The pilot's job when in the air
    •   Hot air rises
    •   The balloon rises into the sky

Unit 4 Let's persuade!

> I can understand how readers are engaged by persuasive writing.

> I can identify key words and phrases in adverts.

Adverts

Fish-tastic!

Do you find breakfast cereals boring?

Then you need to try our brand new, exciting cereal.

FISHY FUN FLAKES!

These are too good to miss!

Our new cereal brings together fun **and** healthy eating.

Fishy Fun Flakes provide the recommended daily amounts of fish oils for developing brains and still taste delicious!

Try a free sample pack!

www.fishyfunflakes.com

Helpful hints

Non-fiction texts have their own special features. The advert here includes:

- a **bold title** – to draw the reader's attention
- **questions** to the reader – to engage them and get them interested in the cereal
- **alliteration** such as *Fishy Fun Flakes* – giving the reader something catchy to remember
- a **brightly coloured picture** – to attract the reader's attention
- **information** about the product shown in a positive light – parents will want to buy it for their children as it helps brain development.

Homophones

Helpful hints

Homophones are words that sound the same but have different meanings and spellings. For example:

write (when you write something on paper)	right (when you are correct or the opposite of left)
stare (when you look at something or someone for a long period of time)	stair (part of a staircase to get up or down between levels in a building)
hare (a rabbit-like creature)	hair (what grows on top of your head)
bare (when something is uncovered)	bear (grizzly animal)
hoarse (when you have a croaky voice)	horse (a four-legged animal you can ride)

1 The advert on page 52 uses a range of ways to engage the reader. Write an example from the advert for each of the following:
  a play on words (a new word which sounds like one you have heard before)
  b alliteration
  c a rhetorical question
  d a hook to engage the reader to find out more.

2 For each of the homophones listed below, use a dictionary to find the meaning of both spellings.
  a creak / creek
  b knead / need
  c allowed / aloud
  d cereal / serial
  e affect / effect

Did you know?

Companies have to make sure that their adverts do not upset children or make them want to buy things that are bad for them such as lots of sugary foods and drinks.

Facts and opinions

1 Copy each of the sentences below. Write (in brackets) whether you think each one is a **fact** or an **opinion**.

a   The leaf was green.
b   The boy had lost his gloves.
c   My house is the best one in the street.
d   It's not much fun playing in the rain.
e   The school won the football competition.
f   I believe that I can be the best football player in the world.

Glossary

fact: something that is known and can be or has been proved to be true

opinion: a view or judgement that is formed about something, it does not have to be based on either facts or knowledge

2 Write down two facts and two opinions about your school. Then write down two facts and two opinions about food.

Talk Partners

Present your facts and opinions about school to a partner. Listen to their facts and opinions. Do you agree? Discuss the ideas further and think about how to deal with ideas different from your own. Next present your facts and opinions about food. Discuss your partner's facts and opinions in the same way.

Leaflets

What is Zany Zoo?

Zany Zoo offers an exhilarating, exciting and energetic day for the whole family. It is situated in Tantown, only 5 miles from the M95 motorway.

There is just so much to ZOO! As well as a huge range of animals from ants to Giant Pandas we have activities scheduled every day with hours of indoor and outdoor fun for all ages!

This year also sees the introduction of our new and exciting PIRATE COVE. You can ride a real pirate ship and search for hidden treasure! Can you really afford to miss out on all the animal (and pirate) fun?

Book online and save money on the entry price.

Helpful hints

Companies produce leaflets to advertise their attractions. Some features of this type of advert are:

- clear, bold heading giving the name of the attraction
- facts about the attraction, such as what visitors can expect to see
- photographs of features – including pictures of other visitors enjoying themselves
- prices or details about where to find these, such as on a related website
- reviews or quotes from previous visitors
- special offers, such as money-off coupons with the leaflet, special family deals
- key contact information, e.g. address, phone number, travel details, website, e-mail address.

1 Write down an example of each of the following from this leaflet:

- a   a rhetorical question
- b   a play on words
- c   a fact
- d   something new to attract visitors.

Glossary

schedule: a list of intended activities and plans

Spelling rules

2 The word 'zoo' has a long vowel phoneme **oo**.

a   Identify words in the leaflet on page 55 that have a long vowel phoneme **ee** or **oo** and make a list. For example, feel or cool.

b   Make a list of the words in the leaflet that have double consonants in them, such as happen or beginning.

c   Identify a rule that can be used to say whether a consonant has to be doubled before a suffix is added.
For example, hide = hidden when 'en' is added.

3 Adverts, such as leaflets, have both explicit and implicit meanings. Explicit means that the information is clearly given in the text. Implicit means the writer hints at something they want the reader to pick up on.

a   Write down two things the leaflet on page 55 'explicitly' tells you.

b   Write down one thing that the leaflet 'implies' to the reader

Try this

Using the text on *page 55* as a basis, write a leaflet for a play-park called Play City. Think carefully about:

- what visitors will *see* and *do* at the park
- what is *special* about the park
- who the park is for
- words and phrases which can be used to make the park sound exciting for the customer.

Afterwards, check through your leaflet and underline any words that are spelt incorrectly. Write these words in your spelling journal and practise spelling them correctly.

Convincing the reader

1 Read the leaflet shown below.

Holiday Fun @ the **Zoo**

Bored during the school holidays?

Don't be. Take the guided ferry tour to see our animals of all shapes and sizes.

FUN FUN FUN!!!

When: 24 April 2015

With over 320 species of animals, you are sure to be interested – and even fascinated at times.

The zoo is amazing. You can get up really close and see the animals.

I'll be visiting the zoo every school holiday!

Write an example of each of the following about the zoo:

a   a statement
b   a fact
c   a question
d   an opinion
e   an order.

2 a   Explain whether you have been persuaded to visit the zoo or not.
- Give a main reason for your answer and explain why you have come to this conclusion. Use examples from the leaflet.
- Give further reasons. For example, *I would like to see real giraffes and the zoo has them* or *I find 320 species of animals too many to look at in one day.*

b   Use the information from the leaflet to write three quotes that could be put in the leaflet as if they were from visitors. Are the quotes positive or negative? What might the visitors talk about?

I can identify how the context of writing impacts on the layout and presentation.

Presenting ideas

1 Look at leaflets for a range of different attractions/products (you can view these online or pick up copies from visitor attractions).

a Make a list of the key features of layout and presentation used. For example, look at the headings, pictures, photos, captions, quotes, colours.

b Are there similarities between the leaflets in terms of layout and presentation features?

c What features work well in convincing the reader to visit the attraction?

Helpful hints

When presenting ideas to a listener, you need to group similar content together. For example, if you are giving a presentation about an attraction you need to:

- state where the place is and why they should visit
- give information about the animals and attractions
- give additional information about facilities such as toilets, restaurants etc.
- give a final summary of why they should visit.

2 Choose one of the places that you would like to go to from activity 1 and write a short presentation explaining the following:

a the name of the place

b what the main attractions are

c what else is available, e.g. food and drink

d where it is situated

e the cost or any special deals

f why you have chosen this place to visit.

Talk Partners

Give your presentation to a partner, group or the class. Remember to:

- look at your audience and keep your head up
- speak slowly, clearly and loudly
- keep still – don't fidget.

Letter of complaint

24 Half Moon Avenue
Bridgetown
Barbados

The Manager
The Toy Emporium
Bridgetown
Barbados

20th February 2015

Dear Sir/Madam,

I am writing to complain about the construction set I bought in your shop last week for my son. I chose the most expensive set as it was a special present for my son's birthday. I spent a long time choosing the gift and felt confident that I had bought a quality product.

When my son opened the construction set he was really excited. However, this excitement quickly turned to disappointment when he started to play with the set. Four of the bricks were not made correctly and therefore did not join together. In addition, the flag that slots into one of the bricks was broken clean in half. Furthermore, there were six bricks missing from the set!

As you can imagine, both my son and I are deeply disappointed by all of this. I am writing to ask you to sort out the situation by replacing the set with a brand new one. Also, I would like the shop to give him something else to apologise for almost ruining his birthday.

I look forward to a swift response.

Yours faithfully,
Mrs Indra Sealy

Identifying key words and phrases

1 The suffix 'ing' has been added to some of the words in the letter on page 59. For example, *writing*, *having* and *trying*.
There are two different rules for adding this suffix.
- Remove the **e** and add –**ing**: *write* → *writing*
- Add –**ing**: *jump* → *jumping*

Copy this table:

Remove the 'e' from the root word and add –ing	Simply add –ing to the word
drive → *driving*	*do* → *doing*

Fill your table with words that fit each of the rules. The first one has been done for you. Write 6 pairs of words in each column.

2 Read the letter on page 59.

a What is Mrs Sealy complaining about?
b Do you think the manager should do as she asks? Why/why not?
c Identify two phrases that show how disappointed Mrs Sealy and her son are with the situation.
d Make a list of the connectives used in the letter.

3 What do you think the manager might write back in a letter?

- Will he/she apologise for what has happened?
- What might he/she offer to do in order to put the situation right?

Write his/her letter of reply.
Afterwards, check through your letter and underline any words that are spelt incorrectly. Write these words in your spelling journal and practise spelling them correctly.

I can understand how points are ordered and paragraphs are used to make a clear argument.

I can understand how connectives are used to structure an argument.

Planning a letter of complaint

1 The letter on page 59 has three paragraphs. The first paragraph is used to explain what the complaint is about. The second paragraph gives details about what is wrong with the product. The final paragraph is used to explain what the writer wants the reader to do about the situation.

a Write a paragraph plan for a complaint about a product. Choose a toy or game that you own and pretend that it is broken, not working properly or missing some pieces. Make notes about what you would include in each paragraph using the following ideas:

• state what the toy is and what the problem is

• explain why you are so disappointed with it

• what do you want the person receiving the letter to do about it to make it better?

2 Look back at your list of connectives from activity 2 on page 60. Add these connectives to your plan from activity 1 above.

Helpful hints

A **connective** is a word or phrase used to link other words or phrases together. For example, *and* or *but*.
When writing an argument text, connectives such as 'furthermore' and 'additionally' can help to emphasise points. *Furthermore, there are six bricks missing from the set!*

Writing letters of complaint

Talk Partners

Use your plan from activity 3 on page 61 to take part in a role-play with a partner. Pretend your partner is the manager and that you are complaining to them about the product in person.

a   Structure your argument. For example:
  * talk first about what the problem is
  * explain why you are so disappointed
  * state what you would like the manager to do about it.

b   Ask your partner to give answers to your points. You might have to adapt your complaint because of his/her responses. So, if the manager says they will try to mend the toy, are you going to continue to ask for a new one or accept what the manager says?

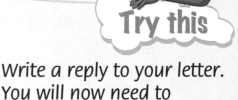

Writing presentation

Write your letter of complaint, using your plan from page 61. Think carefully about the layout and presentation of the letter. Use the example on page 59 to help you. Your letter should have:
* your address in the top right-hand corner
* the address of the person that you are writing to under your own address on the left-hand side of the page
* the date under the person's address
* *Yours faithfully* at the end if you don't know the exact name of the person you are writing to, e.g. *Dear Sir/Madam*
* *Yours sincerely* at the end if you know the name of the person you are writing to, e.g. *Dear Mr Adibi*

Try this

Write a reply to your letter. You will now need to pretend to be the manager. Think about:
* whether it is your fault and whether you will apologise
* what you will offer in order to make the situation right
* anything else that you would like to offer to make the person writing the letter visit your toyshop again.

Non-fiction texts

 There are a wide variety of non-fiction texts.

	Layout features	Presentation features
Persuasive texts	persuasive language to convince the reader to a particular point of view	leaflets/adverts: bright colours, bold headings letters: complaint, response, contact details
Newspaper reports	lead paragraph, main body of report has quotes from observers, conclusion	written in columns, photographs with captions, headline
Explanation texts	opening paragraph, series of paragraphs to explain a process	heading (sometimes a question), paragraphs in time order, sometimes a labelled diagram
Report texts	series of paragraphs related to report	series of paragraphs related to a specific topic

Text 1
Yesterday a man from Ohio phoned the emergency services when he walked into his kitchen to make a cup of coffee and found an alligator sitting in the middle of the floor!

Text 2
I am writing to complain about the wooden chair that I bought from your shop last week …

Text 3
Do you want to add sparkle to your wardrobe? Have you had enough of dull, boring clothes?

Text 4
Howler's is a new and exciting theme park for all ages. With something for all the family, can you afford to miss out?

Identifying non-fiction

1 Look at the texts on page 63 and write down which one of the texts is the following:

a   an advert for a product   b   a letter of complaint
c   an advert for an attraction   d   a newspaper report

2 Copy and complete the following table:

Text type	Language features	Presentation/layout features
Written advert		
Letter of complaint		

Write each statement in the table to show the language and presentation/layout features for each of the text types.

First paragraph states what the product/item is

Textual connectives to link points

Rhetorical questions

Final paragraph states what needs to be done

Bold headings

Address in top right-hand corner

Colourful pictures

Second paragraph states what the problem is

Facts and opinions about the product/ service

Emotive language

Address of the receiver on the left-side of the page

Persuasive language

What have I learnt?

You have been looking at persuasive non-fiction texts that try to convince other people of an opinion or fact. Can you:

● remember some of the different types of non-fiction texts?
● name some of the layout features of a non-fiction text?
● remember some of the language features of a non-fiction text?
● name some connectives in persuasive texts used to emphasise points?

Key facts

Read this newspaper report:

FASCINATING FACTS

Today saw the opening of a new dinosaur museum 'DINO-WORLD' in the city of Kochi. The mayor of the city was there to cut the ribbon and declare the new visitor attraction open. Local schoolchildren were among the first guests to **surge** forward and enter the new building.

The **curator** of the museum said, "We are really thrilled to see so much enthusiasm for our work. This is the **culmination** of many years of planning and we are really delighted it is finally open!"

The museum houses a really big collection of life-size dinosaur models, dinosaur skeletons and stories of other really big prehistoric animals that roamed the earth many millions of years ago. It includes lots of hands-on experiences. These include brass rubbings of dinosaur footprints, a **T-Rex** virtual suit where the wearer is able to see the world through the eyes of a T-Rex and many more really good **interactive displays**.

With a really well-stocked gift shop and café, the reaction of visitors was a really big thumbs up. Mariyah, aged 9, said, "This is the best museum I have ever been to. I really want to come every weekend!"

Glossary

surge: a sudden powerful movement

curator: a museum keeper

enthusiasm: enjoyment, interest or approval

culmination: the highest point of something that has been worked at for a long time

interactive displays: displays where the visitor is invited to respond to it in some way

T-Rex: a type of dinosaur called Tyrannosaurus Rex. It was a meat eater and vicious predator of many other dinosaurs.

I can make short notes from a text and use these to help with my writing.

I can use the correct presentation and layout features for the text I am writing.

I can identify alternative words for overused words and expressions.

Finding key facts

1 Look at the text on page 65 and write down the key facts. For example: What opened? Who opened the museum? Who was at the opening? What is there to do? Where is the mueum?

2 Read through the newspaper report again. The word 'really' is overused throughout. Use a thesaurus to help you make a list of other words that can be used in its place.

3 Use your thesaurus to find alternative words for the following:
- new
- said
- lots

Now put your alternative words in alphabetical order.

4 Rewrite each line of the newspaper report where the word 'really' is used. Use one of your alternative words or phrases. Make sure that your alternative makes sense and has the same meaning. For example, the word 'very' is a synonym for 'really' and would make sense in the following sentence: *With a very well-stocked gift shop …*
You might decide not to write an alternative for the word 'really' but simply to take it out of the sentence altogether.

Writing an advert

1 When writing an advert, you need to include only the key information, as it needs to be eye-catching without too much writing. Use the key facts about DINO-WORLD from the text on page 65 to create an advert **aimed at children**. You can make up some information of your own. The words below give clues to the other features you could include.

> quotes   facts
> alliteration   questions   slogan
> details about other animals
> fun activities

2 Read through your advert from activity 1. Make sure it contains the key layout, language and presentation features you identified during your work on page 64.

Helpful hints

When looking at adverts, you will notice they often have a picture, a slogan or headline with small amounts of writing. Adverts appear colourful and eye-catching through the use of images, coloured writing and borders. The advert needs to include the following language and layout features:

- **adjectives** to describe the product in a positive way
- **facts** about the product
- **opinions** about the product (quotes from users)
- **questions** to make the reader think about whether they need to own the product
- **bold headings** to catch the reader's attention
- **slogans** – a catch line or phrase that will help the reader remember the product.

Try this

Write your advert again, but this time aim it at adults. Think carefully about what they might be interested in and how this would change your advert. The words in the bubble below will give you ideas.

> parking   café   toilets   safety   cost   gift shop
> food   wet-weather activities   how to plan the day

Unit 5 Story settings and characters

Character descriptions

Boggis was a chicken farmer. He kept thousands of chickens. He was enormously fat. This was because he ate three boiled chickens **smothered** with dumplings every day for breakfast, lunch and supper.

Bunce was a duck and goose farmer. He kept thousands of ducks and geese. He was a kind of **pot-bellied** dwarf. He was so short his chin would have been underwater in the shallow end of any swimming-pool in the world. His food was doughnuts and goose-livers … This diet gave him a tummy-ache and a **beastly** temper.

Bean was a turkey and apple farmer. He kept thousands of turkeys in an **orchard** full of apple trees. He never ate any food at all … He was as thin as a pencil and the cleverest of them all.

In the hole lived **Mr Fox** and Mrs Fox and their four Small Foxes.

Extracts from Fantastic Mr Fox by Roald Dahl

Helpful hints

A **character** is a person or animal involved in a story. When reading a story we find out about the characters from the details the writer gives us.

Glossary

smothered: completely covered with

pot-bellied: having a large, round belly that sticks out

beastly: very unpleasant

orchard: a piece of enclosed land that has fruit trees in

I can investigate how characters are built up from details in the text.

I can explore implicit and explicit meanings in a text.

Character role-play

1 Read the character descriptions on page 68. Write down one explicit feature you are told about each character.

  a Boggis   b Bunce   c Bean

Now put the names of the characters into alphabetical order.

2 Write down what the writer wants you to infer about each of the characters. For example, the writer tells us that Boggis was 'enormously fat'. We can infer from this that he is not very fit and cannot run very fast to catch foxes.

  a Write down one implicit feature about Bunce.
  b Write down one implicit feature about Bean.
  c Does the author want you to like the characters? Give a reason for your answer.

3 Draw a picture of a character from page 68. Use the explicit details you have been given and those that you can infer to create a picture of what you think the character looks like. Add labels to your drawing to show the details.

Helpful hints

When acting a character role from a book, you need to identify the key details from the text. For example, what the character looks like, says and whether they are 'good' or 'bad'.

You then think about how they would speak and move. Look at words in the text that show how they spoke, e.g. *muttered, shouted*.

Also look at words that describe their movement and think about their appearance, e.g. *sprinted* or *lumbered*.

Remember there will be explicit details about the character and implicit details about the character that we can infer.

Apostrophes

I can use an apostrophe to show that something belongs to someone or something (possession).

Helpful hints

Apostrophes are small curved marks that hang between certain letters. They are used in two ways to show:

- where letters are missing in contracted words, e.g. could not: couldn't.
- that something belongs to someone or something, e.g. the <u>boy's</u> coat. These are called possessive apostrophes. Look at the table below to see more examples of possessive apostrophes.

For singular nouns and plural nouns that DON'T END with an 's' the apostrophe is added and then the letter 's':
The hat that belongs to the girl = The girl's hat The core in the centre of the Earth = The Earth's core The park belonging to the children = The children's park
For plural nouns that END IN 's' the apostrophe goes after the word:
The tent that belongs to the boys = The boys' tent The food that belongs to the animals = The animals' food

1 Add an apostrophe in the correct place to each of these sentences:
- a The mans umbrella.
- b The princes toothbrush.
- c The wolves food.
- d The cars bonnet.
- e The childrens house.

2 Write each of these sentences using apostrophes to show possession:
- a The bag belongs to the lady.
- b The basket belongs to the cat.
- c The toys belonging to the dogs.
- d The room belonging to the teachers.
- e The barn belonging to the sheep.
- f The car belonging to the men.

Role-play

1 Choose one of the story characters from the picture and make some notes using the table below to show what you think the character would be like in appearance and personality. What would they like and dislike?

A Princess

Wolf

A brave Prince

Helpful hints

Speech marks are used around a quotation or speech to show what a character has said. For example, *"I heard a terrible noise!" said the girl. "What could it be?" asked the boy.*

My character		
Appearance	Personality	Likes/Dislikes

Talk Partners

Find a partner who has a different story character from you. Make up a short (2 minute) drama using your two characters.

a   Introduce yourselves to each other and talk about an event/place that you have both been to, e.g. a party, a show, a park.

b   Think carefully about the way that you speak and move.

c   Share your drama with another pair.

2 Write each of these sentences in direct speech using speech marks.

a   The princess said she was pretty. *"I am pretty," said the princess.*

b   The wolf said he was very hungry.

c   The prince shouted he was very brave.

d   I'm fed up of being a princess said the princess.

e   I like eating old ladies the wolf snarled.

f   I am good at rescuing princesses boasted the prince.

I can write a character profile to capture the reader's imagination.

Character profile

1 Use the ideas from activity 1 on page 71 to create your own story character. Write the following headings and then add notes about your character under each heading:

> **Type of character:** (animal, human, made-up creature)
> What my character is like (personality: shy, scary, happy)
> **Name of character:**
> What my character looks like:
> What my character likes doing:
> What my character doesn't like doing:
> Friends/family related to my character:
> Any special skills or knowledge my character has:

Helpful hints

A character profile gives a description of their personality as well as background details about them. The profile includes:

- details about appearance (hair colour, skin colour, clothes worn)
- some details about related characters (family members)
- their personality (are they fun, angry, happy, loud?)

2 Write a paragraph about your character (a character profile) to show the key details you have planned in activity 1. Use the following structure to help you:

- introduce your character (who they are, type of character, who they are related to in the story)
- what they look like and what their personality is like
- what the character likes doing/doesn't like doing
- information about any key skills.

Talk Partners

With a partner, role play the character from activity 1. Asks questions such as: *What do you like? What do you like doing? What is your personality?*

Prefixes and suffixes

Helpful hints

- **Prefixes** are morphemes that are added to the **beginning** of a word to create a new one. For example, mis- added to the word 'take' becomes **mis**take, so the prefix mis- means wrong.
- **Suffixes** are morphemes added at the **end** of a word to form a new word. The new word that is formed is often from a different word class (a noun can become an adjective when a suffix is added). For example, –less added to the end of the word 'help' (which is a verb or noun) becomes help**less** (which is an adjective). The prefix '-less' means without.

Glossary

morpheme: a meaningful unit of a language that cannot be further divided

1 Draw the table and then write 3 words in each column that use the prefix or suffix shown without any change to the root word (the word that you are adding the prefix or suffix to).

PREFIXES			SUFFIXES		
mis-	**dis-**	**for-**	**-less**	**-ful**	**-ing**
means 'wrong'	means 'not' or 'opposite'	means 'before'	means 'without'	means 'having' or 'giving' or 'quantity that fills'	means 'activity'
mislead	disappoint	forgiven	helpless	playful	playing

2 When a root word ends in a 'y' or an 'e' with a consonant before it, the spelling has to be changed to an 'i' before the suffix is added.

root		suffix		new word
happy	+	ness	=	happiness
happy	+	-ly	=	happily.

Write the correct spelling of the following words when the suffix is added:

a   greedy + ly =
b   easy + ly =
c   carry + ed =
d   happy + er =
e   supply + es =
f   marry + ed =
g   rely + ed =

Setting descriptions

TEXT 1

Trewissick seemed to be sleeping beneath its grey, slate-tiled roofs, along the narrow winding streets down the hill. Silent behind their lace-curtained windows, the little square houses let the roar of the car bounce back from their **whitewashed** walls. Then Great Uncle Merry swung the wheel round, and suddenly they were driving along the edge of the harbour, past water rippling and flashing golden in the afternoon sun.

Over Sea, Under Stone by Susan Cooper

TEXT 2

It was quite a small room, with heavy black beams in the ceiling. By daylight it was amazingly dirty. The stones of the floor were stained and greasy, ash was piled within the **fender**, and the cobwebs hung in dusty droops from the beams. There was a layer of dust on the skull. Sophie absently wiped it off as she went to peer into the sink beside the workbench. She shuddered at the pink and grey slime in it and the white slime dripping from the pump above it.

Howl's Moving Castle by Diana Wynne Jones

Helpful hints

The **setting** is where the story takes place. There may be more than one setting in a story. The author creates a picture of the setting though the details they give in the text. For example, they might give details about what it looks like: *The tall, stone castle sat grandly on top of the hill.*

Glossary

whitewashed: walls that have been painted white

fender: a low frame around a fireplace to stop the coals falling out

Setting details

1 **Explicit** means details that are stated in the text. For example, *grey, slate-tiled roofs.* **Implicit** means details you can infer from the details given. For example, *Trewissick seemed to be sleeping* implies it is quiet and that there aren't people around.

a Read Text 1 and draw a detailed picture of the scene. Use the details given by the author.

b Add labels to the scene to mark the key details. Circle those that show explicit details.

2 Read Text 2. Copy and complete the table below to show whether the details are explicit or implicit in the text.

Text example	Implicit or explicit?
The room was quite small.	
At night it was dark.	
The room was dirty.	
Cobwebs hung from the beams.	
Spiders lived in the room.	
The room had not been cleaned for a long time.	

3 Think about a setting of a place that you know well, such as a room in your house, school or somewhere else you go in your free time. Write a list of things that you could tell your reader about the place (explicit details) and then another list of features that you would like them to infer about the place (implicit details). For example:

Explicit details	**Implicit details**
How big is the room?	How can you show it is a friendly place?
What is on the walls?	How often is it cleaned?

Verbs and adverbs

Text 1
The Chase
Scrambling hastily, the boy climbed up the rock face. He dared to take a brief look down and gulped; it was a very long way down. He had managed to get as far as he had purely on the **adrenalin** of the chase. Now he would have to go on or wait to be rescued … or worse, caught by his attackers.

Text 2
The Race
… As he came into the final straight, he was neck and neck with his biggest **rival**. Was he going to lose out again? He couldn't: he was determined to win. He fixed his eye hard on

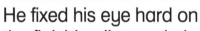

the finishing line and pleaded with his body to go even faster. His body surged forward … he was crossing the line … as CHAMPION!

 Look at the two texts. Make a list of the verbs and adverbs used. Look at your list of verbs and underline 3 powerful verbs.

I can choose and compare verbs to strengthen my writing.

I can identify adverbs and how they add extra detail to the verb.

Verbs and adverbs

2 For each verb below, write down three or more 'powerful verbs' that could be used instead to add excitement, interest or detail to your writing. Use a thesaurus to help you if necessary.

a ran
b walk
c smile
d flew

Now put all the powerful verbs into alphabetical order.

3 For each of the verbs above, choose one of the powerful verbs and write a sentence using it.
For example, a synonym for 'ran' is 'sprinted', so the sentence could be:
He sprinted to the line.
Write four sentences, one for each example above.

4 Using 'The Race' from page 76 as a basis, write a short paragraph in the first person (using I) as if you are winning the race.
Use powerful verbs in your paragraph to show your determination to win. For example, *I was determined to win* or *I sprinted to the line.*

Prefixes and suffixes

Helpful hints

- Refer to the Helpful hints box on page 73 to revise how to use **prefixes** and **suffixes**.
- **Vowels** are speech sounds that are made by the vocal cords. They are also types of letters in the alphabet: **a, e, i, o** and **u.** Short vowels are r<u>a</u>m, l<u>e</u>d, t<u>i</u>p, n<u>o</u>t, r<u>u</u>n. This means they make a short sound when read aloud.

1 Copy and complete the table. Write three words in each column which use the prefix or suffix shown without any change to the root word. In the row below each list, write what the suffix or prefix means.

SUFFIX/PREFIX	PREFIXES			SUFFIXES	
	in-	sub-	pre-	-ness	-er
Examples:	inform	submarine	prefix	kindness	worker
Meaning of suffix/prefix:					

Rule 1: When a root word is one syllable long, has one short vowel and one consonant at the end, the final consonant is doubled when you add a suffix starting with a vowel.
For example: slip + ing = slipping.

Rule two: When a root is one syllable long, has one short vowel, and a suffix is added beginning with a consonant, the root word does not change.
For example: wet + ness = wetness

Try this

For each of the following, write down the final spelling of the word with the suffix added. Think carefully about the rules above:
a   ram + ing =
b   tip + ing =
c   run + ing =
d   run + er =
e   help + less =
f   hot + er =

I can understand how descriptive and expressive language creates mood.

I can elaborate on basic information with some detail.

Using language to create mood

1 Read the texts on pages 74 and 76 again. For each text below, write a sentence explaining the mood that is created through the text. How does it make you feel? Look for clues in the setting to help you with your answer.

a   Over Sea, Under Stone
b   Howl's Moving Castle
c   The Chase
d   The Race

Helpful hints

When creating the mood in stories, authors choose their words carefully and often establish this through the setting they describe.
A setting can be described in different ways to show the mood:

- *cloudy skies, no sun, sounds of rumbling thunder in the distance* would suggest a downcast, unhappy mood.

- *sun shining, fluffy clouds, sounds of laughter in the distance* would suggest a happy mood.

2 Look back at your plan of a setting in activity 3 on page 75.

a   Think about the mood you want to create for your setting. How do you want the reader to feel about the place?
b   Write a list of words and powerful verbs you could use to help the reader feel the mood. Here are some moods with words to get you started.

Spooky
chilling wind, silence, creaking floorboards, shadows on the wall, darkness

Mysterious
doors creaking, intense heat, silence

Frightening
thunder and lightening, wind banging doors, creaking trees, darkness

Warm
sun shining, fluffy clouds, happy sounds in the distance, splashing water

Cold
snow, biting wind, cloudy sky, no sun

Happy
sun shining, fluffy clouds, happy sounds, families playing, ducks quacking

Homophones

I can identify homophones in texts.

The night road up two the castle on his shiny black hoarse. He had defeated the dragon under a blazing son, and was now ready to meat the Princess. He was going to be aloud to marry her. He did not have to weight any longer; he would become a prints at last.

As he looked up at the castle he saw the beautiful princess. Her hare was glistening in the son, it was held in place with a beautiful flour clip. He would, at last, be aloud to speak to her. He tied up his hoarse and ran up the stares to wear the princess was …

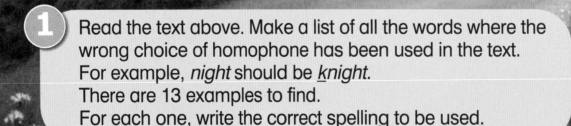

1 Read the text above. Make a list of all the words where the wrong choice of homophone has been used in the text.
For example, *night* should be <u>*knight*</u>.
There are 13 examples to find.
For each one, write the correct spelling to be used.

Homophone confusion

2 Rewrite the text on page 80 using the correct choice of homophone. Share your work with a partner.
Use a dictionary to find the meaning of each incorrect homophone on page 80.
How do these wrong choices make the text funny?

3 Choose three examples of homophones from the text on page 80 and draw two images to show the meaning of each spelling. For example, knight (draw a picture of a man in armour) and night (draw a picture of a dark sky with stars). Write the spelling of each above the correct picture.

I can explore different ways of planning parts of stories.

Writing a setting

1 Look back at the notes you have made about a familiar setting in activity 3 on page 75 and activity 3 on page 79. You should have:

a   a list of explicit details you want to give your reader

b   a list of implicit details you want your reader to infer

c   a note about the mood you want to create

d   a list of powerful verbs (and adverbs) you can use to create the mood.

The final part of your planning is to choose a character you want to introduce into your setting. You are NOT writing a character description. Your character needs to be doing something in your setting, e.g. climbing a rock face or running in a race. Make a note of:

•   your character's name

•   what they look like

•   what they are doing in the setting you have created.

Writing presentation

Use all of the planning in activity 1 to write a detailed setting description (with your character doing some action within it). Think carefully about what to put in your description. Make sure you include:

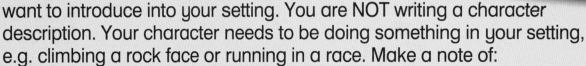

•   what the setting looks like

•   details about smells and sounds

•   details to help your reader understand the mood you wish to create

•   what your character is doing within the setting

•   something the character says, using speech marks.

Editing my work

1 Read your setting description from page 82. Make any changes you want to improve it. This is called editing your work. Check the following:

a   the punctuation (Have you written in clear sentences and used a range of punctuation accurately?)

b   the verbs and adverbs (Have you used powerful verbs and adverbs to describe any action that is taking place?)

c   the grammar (Do all the sentences make sense?)

d   the handwriting (Have you used joined up writing throughout?)

e   the spelling (Underline any words that are spelt incorrectly. Write the correct spelling of the word above. Add these words to your spelling journal and practise spelling them correctly.)

Now rewrite your edited version with improvements.

2 Draw an illustration to go with your setting description. This needs to show the explicit details you have included as well as extra details to help the reader to make inferences about the mood.

Talk Partners

Give your illustration to a partner and then read the description to them. Does the illustration match the description?

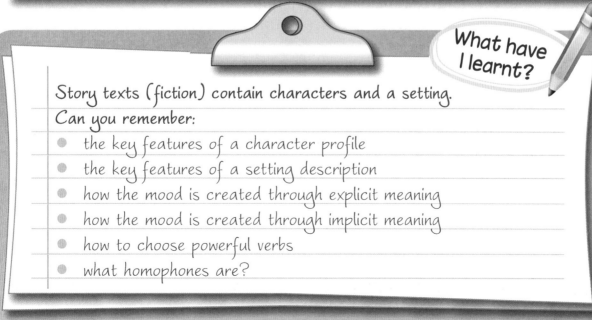

What have I learnt?

Story texts (fiction) contain characters and a setting.

Can you remember:

- the key features of a character profile
- the key features of a setting description
- how the mood is created through explicit meaning
- how the mood is created through implicit meaning
- how to choose powerful verbs
- what homophones are?

Unit 6 Let's act!

Playscripts

Scene 1: *A house with some trees beside it and fields of golden grasses.*

Narrator: Long ago in India there lived a wealthy merchant who was not at all happy with his only son. His mother always thought the best of him, however, and was continually making excuses for him.

(Merchant and Wife enter, speaking to each other)

Merchant: He just doesn't listen. I don't know how he can be my son.

Wife: Don't say that! He's our dear child. He just needs some extra attention.

Merchant: You give him too much attention as it is! Let's face it, the boy is lazy.

Wife: Please, just give him one more chance to prove himself.

Merchant: All right. But that fool is going to have to work for it. He's going to have to think.

(Son enters)

Son: Hello Father and Mother. How are you today?

Merchant: Fine, fine. I have something I want you to do. I will give you one last chance to prove yourself.

Son: What can I do?

Merchant: I am going to give you this paisa. I want you to go to the bazaar and buy something to eat, something to drink, something for the cow to chew on and something to plant in the garden.

Son: How do you expect me to do that with only one paisa? That's not fair!

Merchant: *(with hands on hips)* Lots of things in life aren't fair!

Son: I'll show you, Father. I can do it! *(to audience)* Somehow...

Helpful hints

A **playscript** is a piece of writing in the form of drama. The key features of a playscript are:

- a **title**
- **character list** at the beginning
- the story is broken down into **scenes**
- **characters' names** are on the left with colons after them to show what they say.
- **lines** for each new speaker
- **stage directions** written in the present tense (to tell the actors how to say the lines, move, use the props).

1 In a group of four, read through this playscript. Each person should read a different character.

Narrative order

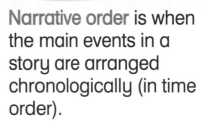

Helpful hints

Narrative order is when the main events in a story are arranged chronologically (in time order).

Scene 2: Inside a house

(Son enters with Ironsmith's Daughter carrying a watermelon)

Son: Here's a watermelon, Father. It provides something to eat, something to drink, something for the cow to chew on and something to plant in the garden.

Merchant: So it does. I'm impressed!

Wife: I knew you could do it, son.

Son: Actually, it was the ironsmith's daughter who had the idea.

Merchant: And you don't take the credit either. That's two good moves. Young lady, how did you think of such a fine solution?

Ironsmith's daughter: Well, the watermelon takes care of all your conditions.

Merchant: Indeed it does. I am proud of you both. Young people! Just when you are ready to give up on them they surprise you! And to think I didn't have any idea myself how to use the paisa to solve the problem...

From All for a Paisa, an Indian folk tale *retold by Elaine L. Lindy and adapted as a playscript by Linsay Parker*

Talk Partners

In your group, read the rest of the playscript and discuss the following:

a   what is the order of events in the playscript on pages 84–85?

b   can you make up a scene for the middle of the playscript, where the son goes to the market, meets the Ironsmith's daughter and buys a watermelon?

Now perform your new scene to another group.

Scene list

Little Red Riding Hood

Scene 1: Little Red Riding Hood's cottage
Characters: Little Red Riding Hood and her mother

Scene 2: In the woods
Characters: Little Red Riding Hood and the wolf

Scene 3: Grandma's cottage
Characters: Grandma and the wolf

Scene 4: Grandma's cottage
Characters: The wolf and Little Red Riding Hood

Scene 5: Grandma's cottage
Characters: The wolf, Little Red Riding Hood, woodcutter and Grandma

Helpful hints

Scenes make up individual parts of a story (they help to show the **narrative order** of the play). The scenes in a play reflect a change in location or characters involved in the action.

Talk Partners

Read through the scene list above. With a partner, retell the story to remind yourself of the narrative. Use the scene titles and information about characters involved to help you.

Glossary

cottage: a small house that is usually in the country

woodcutter: a person who cuts down trees or branches (e.g. to burn as fuel)

I can explore how scenes are built up.

I can understand the main stages in a story.

More about narrative order

1 For each scene on page 86, write a description of the main action that occurs showing what is going to happen. For example, in Scene 1 Little Red Riding Hood agrees to take the cakes to her Grandmother who is feeling unwell.

2 In a group, choose one of the scenes from the story and perform the action. Remember to use your voice and movements to help you act like the character you are portraying.

3 Write a playscript for the scene your group has just performed in activity 2. Use the example on page 84 as well as the notes about key features of playscripts to help you. Think about the improvised version your group created to help you add details to the script.

Afterwards, check through your playscript and underline any words that are spelt incorrectly. Write these words in your spelling journal and practise spelling them correctly.

Reading a playscript

Scene 1: *Inside a village house*

Narrator: Once there was a man who was strong. When he gathered firewood he hauled twice as much as anybody else in the village. This man's name was Shadusa and his wife was named Shettu.

Shadusa: *(boastfully, flexing muscles)* Just look at these muscles. I must be the strongest man in the world. From now on call me Master Man!

Shettu: *(scolding)* Quit your foolish boasting! No matter how strong you are there will always be somebody stronger. And watch out, or someday you may meet him.

Scene 2: *By the edge of a well*

Narrator: The next day Shettu went to a well for a drink. She threw in a bucket and then pulled on the rope. But though she tugged and heaved she could not lift the bucket. Just then a woman walked up with a baby strapped to her back.

Shettu: *(helpfully)* You'll get no water here today. The bucket won't come up.

Woman: Wait a moment.

Narrator: The woman untied her baby and set him on the ground.

Woman: Pull up the bucket for Mama...

Narrator: The baby quickly pulled up the bucket and filled his mother's container. Then he threw in the bucket and pulled it up once more for Shettu.

Shettu: *(gasps)* I don't believe it!

Woman: Oh it's not strange. After all, my husband is Master Man. The baby is just like his father, very strong!

Scene 3: *Back at the village house*

Narrator: When Shettu got home she told Shadusa what happened.

Shadusa: *(furiously)* Master Man? He can't call himself that. I will have to teach him a lesson!

Shettu: *(pleading, holding on to Shadusa's arm)* Oh husband don't! If the baby is so strong, think what the father must be like. You will get yourself hurt!

From Master Man *by Aaron Shepard*

 1 Write down the key details about Shadusa from this playscript. Key details are what he is like, what his relationship to Shettu is and how he speaks to her. What do you feel about him?

I can investigate how characters are built up from details.

I can adapt my speech and gestures to create a character in drama.

Character build up

2 Read the playscript on page 88 again.
a What details do we learn about the baby from the script?
b Why might Shettu be worried about Shadusa meeting the baby's father? Discuss your ideas with a partner.

Talk Partners

In a group, take a part each and practise the scene, using the stage directions (shown in *italics*) to help add detail to your character.

3 In a group of 5 or 6, take it in turns to be in the hot-seat as either Shettu or Shadusa. The other members of the group must ask questions to find out:
- who you are
- what you like
- what you don't like
- how you are feeling about what is going to happen.

Try this

Write the next scene of the story when Shadusa meets the baby's father. Think about:
- What events will take place?
- How will Shadusa speak to the father (crossly, boastfully, etc.)?
- Who is really Master Man at the end of the scene?

Stage directions

1 Re-read the playscript on page 88. Copy and complete this table:

Setting the scene	Telling the character what to **do**	Telling the character how to **speak**

Write examples of each type of stage direction from the playscript on page 88 in the correct column in your table.

2 Look back at the script on page 84. There are some stage directions related to what the characters do and what the scene looks like, but nothing about how the characters speak. Rewrite the playscript adding stage directions to help the actors on how to speak.

3 With a group, perform your additional scene from page 89. Add stage directions on how the characters speak to help you improve the performance. Think about how emotion can be shown both in your voice and actions. For example, to show you are scared you might whisper and say the words slowly, but also shake your body or move away from the threat.

I can read and perform play-scripts.

I can identify differences between reading silently and reading aloud.

Reading aloud and reading silently

1 In your head, read your script from activity 2 on page 90. Make a note of the time it took you to read all of the words. Make sure you read the scene clearly and at the pace you usually read.

2 Read the same script aloud, taking a pause at commas and a brief stop at full stops. Time how long this takes you.
  a Did it take more or less time than reading silently?
  b Why do you think this is?

3 Work with three other learners to perform the playscript, using your stage directions to help bring the characters alive. Include movements of the characters and make up some simple scenery using chairs or tables.
  a What skills do you use when performing that are the same as reading?
  b What additional skills do you use when performing that you don't use when reading?

Helpful hints

Reading **silently** is when you read something in your head. Reading **aloud** is when someone is listening to you. This could be as a performance or simply reading a book to a friend.

Performing a part

Scene: *An ordinary family house at breakfast time. Two children are sitting at the table. Mum is standing at the sink.*

Raj: Mum, I've got a school trip today.

Mum: *(puzzled)* Is that today?

Raj: *(in a raised voice)* Yes! You know it is! We're going to that museum. I need a packed lunch.

Mum: *(crossly)* You're telling me this now?

Senara: Oh, and it's insect day today too!

Mum: *(laughing)* What is insect day?

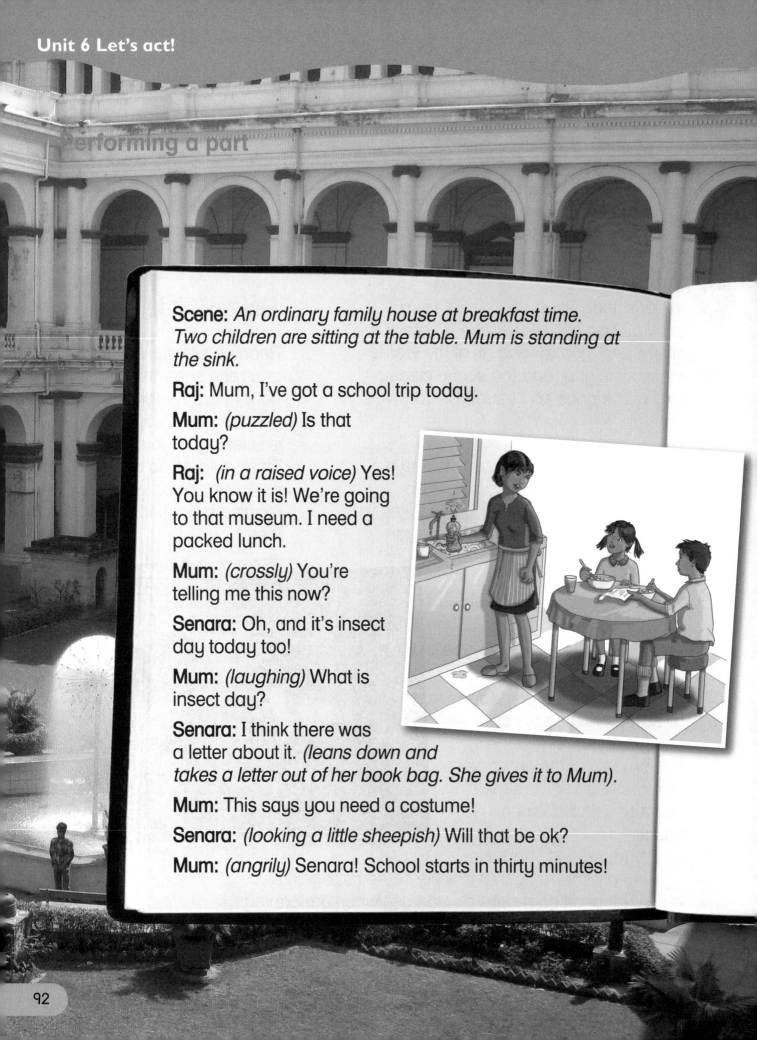

Senara: I think there was a letter about it. *(leans down and takes a letter out of her book bag. She gives it to Mum).*

Mum: This says you need a costume!

Senara: *(looking a little sheepish)* Will that be ok?

Mum: *(angrily)* Senara! School starts in thirty minutes!

Talk Partners

In a group of three, assign parts to each person and then practise the playscript on page 92.

a Think carefully about your voice, facial expression and use the stage directions to help you play your part convincingly.

b Perform your play to the rest of the class or another group. Ask for feedback on how well your characters were portrayed.

1 Think about your own family and what it is like at mealtimes.

a Write a short playscript. Use the ideas from page 92.

b In a small group, perform your playscript.

What have I learnt?

Read back through your playscript. Check that you have:
- used a new line for each new character
- used conventions of a playscript such as colons after character names on the left-hand side
- added stage directions to show the actions characters have to perform as well as how they have to say their lines
- given details about what the scene looks like as well as any props required.

Fiction

Read the extract and answer ALL the questions which follow.

'How much sugar in your tea today, Grandma?' George asked her.

'One spoon,' she said. 'And no milk.'

Most grandmothers are lovely, kind, helpful old ladies, but not this one. She spent all day and every day sitting in her chair by the window. Always complaining, grousing, grouching, grumbling, griping about something or other. Never once, even on her best days, had she smiled at George and said, 'Well how are you this morning, George?' or 'Why don't you and I have a game of Snakes and Ladders?' or 'How was school today?' She didn't seem to care about other people, only about herself. She was a grouchy old grouch.

George went into the kitchen and made Grandma a cup of tea with a teabag. He put one spoon of sugar in it and no milk. He stirred the sugar well and carried the cup into the living-room.

Grandma sipped the tea. 'It's not sweet enough,' she said. 'Put more sugar in.'

George took the cup back to the kitchen and added another spoonful of sugar. He stirred it again and carried it carefully in to Grandma.

'Where's the saucer?' she said. 'I won't have a cup without a saucer.'

George fetched her a saucer.

From George's Marvellous Medicine by Roald Dahl

1   How many spoons of sugar should
    Grandma have asked for at the start?
    Write one answer.   (1)
    a   two
    b   one
    c   three
    d   none

2   What did George want his Grandma to do that she did
    not do? Write two features.   (2)

3   Who did George's grandmother care about most?   (1)

4   Find the sentence *'Never once, even on her best days, had
    she smiled at George ...'.* What is the author demonstrating
    to the reader by using this sentence? Choose one answer
    from the list below.   (1)

    a   Grandma was always smiling on days she felt well.
    b   Grandma never ever smiled.
    c   Grandma smiled at George when she was having
        a good day.
    d   Grandma only smiled at George on good days.

5   Find and copy the adverb used to show how
    George took the tea to Grandma.   (1)

6   Look at the places where Grandma speaks. Copy an
    example from the text to show each type of sentence.

    a   A complaint   (1)
    b   A command   (1)
    c   A question   (1)
    d   A statement   (1)

7   What does the author show us about George's character in
    this extract? Choose three answers from the list below.   (3)

    noisy   obedient   disappointed   kind   angry   rude

Non-fiction

Read the leaflet and answer ALL the questions which follow.

Desert Tours

Experience the desert like you have never seen it before with DAZZLING DESERT TOURS. We promise you will not be disappointed.

Dazzling Desert Tours are ideal if you are fit and thirsty for adventure! The facilities and organisation offered are second to none. All you have to do is enjoy yourself!

We operate within the Sahara desert region. Our superb tours allow you and your party to experience the delights of the desert both on foot and in our secure, reliable vehicles.

For our most popular tour you will spend 5 days in the desert and 4 nights sleeping in bivouacs. During the tour you will be driven in our specially adapted desert vehicles through valleys, villages and open desert. Throughout the five days you will experience camel rides, trekking and many fabulous sights and sounds.

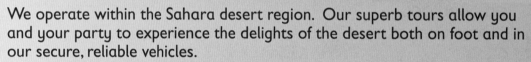

Evenings will be spent in local villages. These places have been selected carefully to ensure maximum safety and enjoyment. Our hosts will welcome you to their villages with open arms. You will be able to enjoy the sounds, sights and smells of real desert life.

So, if you are thinking of visiting the desert, choose us at Dazzling Desert Tours to give you an experience you will never forget. We offer awe, wonder, amazement and fulfilment of dreams.

1 How long do you spend in the desert if you choose the most popular DAZZLING DESERT TOUR?
Choose the correct answer. (1)

   a 4 days   **b** 5 days   **c** 3 days   **d** 6 days

2 Who are DAZZLING DESERT TOURS suited for? (1)

3 Read the fifth paragraph. Write a one sentence summary showing the information it gives. (1)

4 The text includes facts and opinions. Copy each sentence below and write fact or opinion beside it.
   a You have to be fit to go on the tour. (1)
   b The tours will not disappoint you. (1)
   c You will have the chance to ride a camel. (1)

5 Which of these text types is the best description of this leaflet? Choose one answer from the list below. (1)

> fiction   instructions   report   persuasion   explanation

6 What is the purpose of the final paragraph? (1)

7 Find and write three adjectives that are used to help persuade the reader they should go on the tour. (3)

8 Write an advertisement for a visit to a different type of place such as a jungle, rainforest, city or lake. (5)

You will need to decide:
- where you are going to write about
- what you are going to tell people about the place
- why people should visit.

Before you write, think about how you can persuade your reader through:
- the language you use
- the order in which you introduce information
- the opening paragraph
- the final paragraph.

Unit 7 Looking at fiction

Story stages

1 Sort the following sentences into the correct order to show the main stages of a story:

a The headteacher was dangling from the top of the school roof.

b Samrath resolved never to use his special powers on teachers again.

c Once upon a time there lived a boy called Samrath who had special powers.

d Samrath was angry with the headteacher and used his special powers to get revenge.

e The fire service arrived and used a long ladder to rescue the headteacher.

Helpful hints

Narrative order is when the main parts of a story are ordered in chronological (time) order.

There are five main stages to any story:
- introduction
- events leading to the climax
- climax point of the story
- events leading to resolution
- resolution.

2 Read this story plan. It is in the wrong narrative order. Write the letters to show the correct order.

a Daisy is taken to market.

b A woman opens the door for the first time to see Jack standing there.

c Jack becomes a thief.

d The giant falls into the garden.

e Jack is pursued by the giant.

f Jack is sent to bed without any supper.

g The beans grow into an interesting plant.

3 Copy the headings below. Choose a story you know well and write a sentence next to each heading to show the main stages of the story.

- Beginning
- Events leading to conflict/climax
- Conflict/climax
- Events leading to resolution
- Resolution

The swimming lesson

It was in the summer, early in the morning and early in the evening, that the water was just perfect for swimming. My cousins and I would roll up a fresh set of clothes into towels and, in a large, chattering group, walk towards the river.

"What stroke do you want to learn?" a ten-year-old cousin once asked me. He was the swimming champion at school and double my age.

"Any stroke will do," I answered as if I knew what strokes were.

"Well, first you learn how to float and then I'll teach you how to crawl. Now lie flat in my arms and keep your head down."

"Shall I keep my eyes shut?"

"As you want."

I kept my eyes shut. It was not so easy to float.

"Wait," said my cousin.

He swam to the far bank and I saw him disappear in the watermelon fields. Soon he was rolling a large watermelon towards the river. As soon as it hit the water, the giant fruit began to float.

"Hang on to the watermelon with your arms outstretched," my cousin said.

"Keep your head down and kick your legs without bending your knees."

That did it. I was held up by the watermelon and carried downstream by the gentle summer current.

By Madhur Jaffrey

I can find significant events in a story.

Significant events

1 Read the text on page 99.

a Why did the narrator shut her eyes at the start?

b Why does the cousin give the narrator a watermelon?

c How do you think the narrator is feeling at the end of the extract?

Helpful hints

Significant events are the key (or most important) events that happen in the story. They often form the **key parts** of the overall plan for the story.

Talk Partners

With a partner, read the text on page 99 again. Discuss the following questions:

a Which part of the whole story do you think this extract is from? Why?

b What significant events have happened already in the story? Why?

c What do you think might happen next? Why?

2 Use the headings below to write down a plan for the story on page 99. Depending on your discussion, you will need to make up the climax point, events leading to resolution and resolution stages of the story. Include the ideas from the discussion with your partner.

- Introduction (e.g. what happens in the first paragraph)
- Events leading to climax (significant events in the story so far)
- Climax point of the story (what happens after the narrator is carried downstream)
- Events leading to resolution (how the narrator is rescued from the situation in the climax)
- Resolution (how the story ends)

Character profiles

1 Choose a character from a book. Copy the table below and write down notes to show the key details about the character. Some of these you will know from the story and others you will need to make up.

Name	
Age	
Looks (adjectives)	
Lives	
Eats	
Likes	
Dislikes	

Helpful hints

Remember! A **character profile** gives the reader key details about the character, including:

- name and age
- adjectives to describe his/her looks
- where the character lives
- what the character eats
- the character's likes and dislikes.

Talk Partners

Use the character from activity 1 to take part in a 'hot seat' activity with a partner. Sit in the hot seat and pretend to be your character. Ask your partner to find out as much as possible about your character by questioning you for one minute. Try to stay in role as the character throughout. Then swap so that your partner is in the 'hot seat'.

2 Write a short character profile about the character from activity 1. Try to write no more than 100 words and explain the key details you have identified and expanded on in your talk partner work.

Stone soup

Once upon a time there was a terrible shortage of food in the land. People hid the few things they had and did not share with their neighbours.

One day a stranger arrived in a village. He greeted the people and said, "I am looking for a soft bed to sleep tonight and I need a place to have a meal."

The people said, "There is not a bite to eat in the whole village. We are all hungry here. You better move on."

"I don't need food," the stranger said, "I have my own. In fact, I am going to make a pot of stone soup to share with all of you."

He took out an iron pot and filled it with water. Then he made a fire and set the water to boil. The stranger felt in his pockets and took out a smooth, round stone. He dropped this into the water.

Next, with many people watching, the stranger tasted the stone soup and licked his lips. The people moved closer, hoping to get a taste.

"Ahh," the stranger said loudly to himself. "This is tasty. Of course, it would be better with a little onion and perhaps some salt and pepper."

A woman gave the stranger a small onion she had been hiding.

A man brought some salt and pepper. The stranger added these to the pot.

The stranger tasted the soup again. "This is delicious," he cried.

"Of course, it would be better if we added some meat bones."

The village butcher managed to find a shin bone, the stranger added it to the soup.

The stranger kept on tasting the soup and saying what would make it better. The villagers found some potatoes, carrots and barley. These all went into the stone soup.

In the end, there was a delicious meal for everyone in the village to share.

Personal response

1 Read the text on page 102. Answer these questions.

a Why were people hiding their food?

b How were the people feeling at the start of the story?

c What do you think the people said to the man when he started to make the soup?

d How did the man get the people to give him their hidden food?

e Do you think the man tricked the people? Write a short paragraph explaining your thoughts about the man's actions.

Try this

Rewrite the sentences below, adding commas where they are required.

a The villagers who were terribly hungry hid their food.

b The stranger was a kind clever man.

c The stranger took out a pot, made a fire and set the water to boil.

d The people wanted to taste the soup.

e In the end there was a big delicious pot of soup to share.

Helpful hints

A **comma** is a punctuation mark that can be used to break up parts of a sentence into smaller parts. Here are a few examples of how they can be used.

• To separate two adjectives in a sentence where the word *and* could be used: *He is a happy, friendly man.*

• In the place of brackets to separate the extra information:
The two men, who were brothers, walked to the shop.

• Between clauses (a clause is a short sentence that could stand alone):
My favourite colour is blue, but my friend's favourite colour is red.

Did you know?

The story of the stone soup is a fable. Fables are old stories that are passed down from parents to children. Fables teach a moral lesson. The moral of this story is that when everyone works together and does what good they can, they achieve great things.

Using speech marks

1 Copy the sentences below, adding speech marks in the correct places:

a STOP shouted the teacher!

b Please can you help me asked the boy.

c The lady asked how old are you?

d Welcome to our school said the headteacher.

e The girl whispered come to my party tomorrow.

2 Write each of the following examples into direct speech:

a The lady said that she was very hungry.

b The boy shouted loudly that he was proud to have won the competition.

c The teacher told the boy to listen carefully to her instructions.

d Jack told his mother that he had swapped the cow for some beans.

e The man whispered that he was frightened of spiders.

f The lady said thank you to everyone.

Helpful hints

Dialogue is a conversation between two or more people. When dialogue is written in texts, it is usually in the present tense and uses speech marks. For example,

"I like chocolate cake,"
said Anne.

Speech marks surround the dialogue, also called **direct speech**, in a text. There is usually a capital letter at the start of dialogue within speech marks.

3 Continue the dialogue below to show what Pedro is doing today. Make sure Pedro asks Peter a question so that each character speaks once (or more if you want to challenge yourself).

"Hello Peter, how are you today?" asked Pedro.
"I'm fine, thank you! What are you doing today?" replied Peter.

Spelling patterns

1 Refer to the Helpful hints box. Read each word in the lists below and then write down the odd one out in each group:

a boot, foot, hoot, loot, root
b love, glove, cove, dove
c enough, plough, tough
d match, catch, snatch, watch, hatch
e crow, flow, now, blow, below
f through, plough, bough
g eight, weight, height
h one, bone, cone, stone

Helpful hints

A **letter string** is a sequence of letters forming a phoneme or a morpheme. Some words that have the same letter string are pronounced differently. For example, love and move or soot and hoot.

2 Work with a partner to write a list of 12 words that have the letter string 'ough'.

a Look at your list of words and group them together to show words where the letter strings make the same sound as each other.
b How many different sounds does this letter string make?
c Now put your words into alphabetical order.

3 Write a word that uses the same letter string as in the words below but is pronounced differently:

a l**atch**
b w**ear**
c l**ie**
d y**our**

Sam's Duck

"You'll like it when you get there," said Sam's grandad. "I won't," said Sam. But he knew he had to go to the farm. Everyone in Mrs Southerden's class was going. Besides, Grandad said it would be good for him. "City boy like you can learn a lot down on the farm," he said. "Fresh air, fresh eggs. I wish I could go myself. You'll be back on Friday for my birthday. We'll have a party."

Grandad waved goodbye. Sam watched from the back of the coach 'till he couldn't see him anymore. It was a whole week before he would be home again. Sam did his best not to cry.

It was a very long way to Devon. Motorways turned to roads, roads turned to lanes, narrow lanes with grass growing down the middle. Suddenly ahead of them was a huge house, like a palace, with green fields and trees all around.

Sam's Duck by Michael Morpurgo

Did you know?

Michael Morpurgo was a teacher before he became an author. His book 'War Horse' has been made into a film by Steven Spielberg.

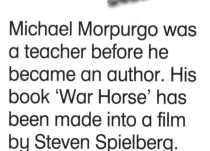

I can use an apostrophe to show that an object belongs to somebody or something.

Possessive apostrophes

1 Draw this table:

Apostrophes for omission	Apostrophes for possession

Read the text on page 106 and find the words that have apostrophes.
Write them into the correct column of the table to show if they have been used for omission or possession.

Helpful hints

Apostrophes are used in the following ways:
- to show where letters are missing (**omission**), also called a **contraction**, *hasn't = has not*
- to show where something belongs to someone (**possession**), *the girl's coat.*

2 Write five more words (not in the text) in each column from activity 1.

3 Write each of these as sentences using an apostrophe to show possession.

a   The pencils belonging to the boy.
   E.g. The boy's pencils.
b   The clothes belonging to the girl.
c   The computer belonging to Hannah.
d   The keys belonging to Imran.
e   The bags belonging to the girls.
f   The books belonging to the children.

I can choose powerful adjectives to make my writing more interesting.

Using adjectives

1 Read through the text on page 106 and write a list of all of the adjectives that are used.

2 The following nouns from the story on page 106 do not have adjectives to describe them. For each one, write two adjectives to show different degrees of intensity. For example, 'the **hot** sun' or the **scorching** sun'.

a   farm
b   class
c   coach
d   road

Helpful hints

A **noun** is a word used to identify a class of people, place or thing (common noun) or to name a particular one (proper noun).

Adjectives are words that describe qualities or characteristics of nouns: *big, blue, fast.*

Sometimes the quality that the adjective describes can vary in intensity, for example the adjective 'hot' could be given an intensity: *boiling, extremely hot, very hot, hot, quite hot, warm …*

Try this

Read some other books by Michael Morpurgo. Here are a few suggestions to get you started:
* Kaspar: Prince of Cats
* Toro! Toro!
* Farm Boy

As you read, look out for adjectives, particularly ones that vary in their intensity. Make a list of these for use in your own writing.

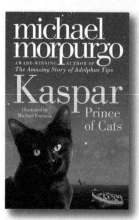

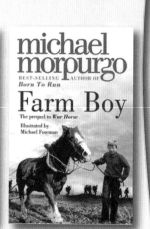

Settings in stories

1 Read the text below and answer these questions:
  a   What was wrong with the front door?
  b   What were 'like shadows in the sunset'?
  c   What made the children stay well away?
  d   What clue shows that someone was living in the house?

The house on the hill

The house was near to falling down – the front door was hanging on one hinge, swinging in the cold winter's wind. It creaked strangely as it swung backwards and forwards, a noise that scared the children in the street into staying well away. Staring blankly, the broken windows caught the rays of the setting sun, making them appear almost orange. The roof of the building had missing tiles here and there and black crows peered down at the people below, like shadows in the sunset. Despite its run-down appearance, a thin trail of smoke drifted from the crooked chimney pot: someone was living there …

Multisyllabic words

1 These words come from the extract on page 109. Write each word showing the syllable break:

a swinging
b winter
c staying
d away
e sunset
f drifted

2
a Find and write the simile used in the extract on page 109.
b Write a simile that improves the following description:
a thin trail of smoke drifted from the crooked chimney pot like …

3 What mood is created by the setting description? Use information from the extract to explain your answer. Make sure that you:
• state the mood that you think is created
• explain how this mood is created. For example, *the creaking door creates a feeling of mystery or friendliness …*

Helpful hints

Remember! **Settings** in stories tell the reader about the place or places where the story takes place. They give information about:
• where the story is set
• what time of day or night the action is taking place
• what the weather is like (this can add to the mood of the story, e.g. stormy skies suggests scary or mystery while sunshine suggests peace and happiness)
• the sounds and smells the characters experience.

A detailed setting description

I can begin to use paragraphs to organise my ideas.

1 Read the setting description on page 109. Close your eyes and imagine you are there. Using the information you are given, as well as your own feelings, make notes about:
  a What would you see if you were standing in front of the house?
  b What sounds would you hear?
  c What smells would you smell?
  d How would you feel with all of these sights, smells and sounds?

2 Plan a detailed setting description (of any setting you want) with three paragraphs. Read the setting description on page 109 again to help you. Use the following headings to make notes about each paragraph in your setting:
  • **Paragraph 1.** Introduce the setting by showing where it is. For example, the house, the park …
  • **Paragraph 2.** Describe the main feature in detail. For example, think about the sights, sounds, smells. While doing this, think about the mood you want to create.
  • **Paragraph 3.** Introduce some action to the setting. For example, a character is doing something within the scene. Think about the impact this particular action has on the setting.

Writing presentation

Using the notes from activity 2, write the paragraphs of your setting description. Read through your work carefully and check spellings in a dictionary. Any words you have spelt incorrectly should be recorded in your spelling journal.

Character profile

Dressed in a dark coat, the man quietly walked into the shop. He was a small man, with dark brown hair, short cut, and a large beard. He was wearing clean grey trousers and shiny black shoes. He picked up a loaf of bread and searched through the pockets of his coat to find some money. A name badge dropped out with the words J.T. Whitton. Without speaking, he picked up the badge, placed the correct change on the counter and turned to leave.

"Thanks … bye," said the shopkeeper, but the man had already gone without a word…

1 Copy and complete this character profile to show what you have found out about the character described above. Write the information you know from the extract in one colour. Write any information you make up from your own inferences/imagination in another colour.

Name	
Age	
Height	
Looks	
Clothes	
Personality	

I know how characters are built up from details.

I can identify key words and phrases in descriptions.

Character descriptions

2 Draw a detailed picture of the image you have of the man from the character description on page 112. Use your character profile from activity 1 to help you. Add labels to show which details are from the text (those written in one colour in your character profile) and those which come from your imagination/inferences (those written in another colour on your character profile).

3 Rewrite the character description from page 112 to create a completely opposite image. For example, a man who is scruffy, loud and chatty. Can you choose words and phrases carefully to create the character mood you want?

What have I learnt?

You have been looking at how characters and settings are built up in stories, as well as the narrative order of stories.

See if you can answer these questions:

- What are the main stages in a story?
- How can you identify a significant event in a story? Which stage does it usually fall into?
- What details are included in a character profile?
- Can you explain the two ways that apostrophes are used in words?

Changing stories into reports

Starting with a story

An interesting discovery ...

"What was that?" Mateo twisted his head quickly in the direction of the sound that had come from the bushes. He stalked closer, treading carefully on the forest floor. He could hear a faint rustling from under the bush.

Lifting the lower branches carefully, Mateo peered into the space below the bush. There, huddled up in a small ball, was a small, furry creature. Two large, round eyes stared up at him. Slowly, the creature unfurled two large, bat-like ears, waggling them playfully. Mateo reached down and put a hand out. The creature lifted itself onto a pair of stubby legs, ending in two small pink feet. Mateo noticed it seemed to have two more pairs of legs which it used to steady itself. What on earth was it? he thought.

Slowly – carefully he reached down and stroked the small creature. It purred loudly at his touch, even rubbing its face against his hand. Mateo was reminded of the way his sister's cat would rub itself against his hand when it wanted to be stroked. He squatted down and scooped the creature up. He could feel a small tail at the back, wagging.

"Do you want to come home with me?" Mateo asked the creature, his face breaking into a wide grin. To his surprise, the creature nodded. It pointed, with two of its arms, towards Mateo's rucksack. This lay on the ground some distance away. Mateo looked at the rucksack, then at the creature, before his grin broadened even further. "I'm going to be famous!" he chuckled, as he picked the creature up and placed it in his rucksack.

I can note the key words and phrases in an extract.

1 Copy the following headings and then write details for each heading based on the story on page 114.
a WHO is it about?
b WHAT has happened?
c WHERE did it happen?
d WHY is it interesting for people to read?

Helpful hints

A **summary** is a short version of the key points within a text. Key words and phrases can be identified by thinking about the main stages of a story:

* beginning
* build up to conflict/climax
* conflict/climax
* events leading to resolution
* resolution

Key words and phrases often identify a move to the next stage or a key event. For example, *the discovery of the creature.*

2 Write two bullet points for each paragraph in the text to show the key points. For example:

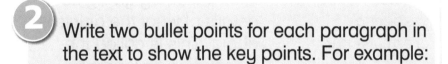

Paragraph 1
* The character of Mateo is introduced
* The setting is introduced.

Try this

Read a 'real' newspaper report or story and highlight the key points and phrases. Think about the questions:
WHO? WHAT? WHY? WHEN? WHERE? when identifying key points.

I can explain how newspaper reports are made interesting for the reader.

Using fiction to plan a report

Look at the plan below for a newspaper report based on the story on page 114.

Orientation paragraph:
Who? Mateo
What? Found a small, furry creature
Where? In bushes in a forest
When? Doesn't say but if it is reported as news it will have happened recently, so can say 'yesterday'
Why? It is an unusual creature and responded to Mateo's questions with gestures.

Main story paragraph:
Mateo discovered a creature which resembled the parts of other known creatures. He discovered it in the forest. The creature appeared friendly and responded to Mateo's question about going home with him. The creature indicated that it wanted to go home in Mateo's rucksack.

Re-orientation paragraph:
Mateo carried the creature home and (called the police/rang the natural history museum/rang the local TV station ...)

Helpful hints

Newspapers are sources of printed information about events that have happened locally, nationally and internationally. Newspaper reports need to engage the reader in the first paragraph so that they continue reading the rest of the report. This first paragraph has to give a summary of the key information by giving key details of what the article is about. This is called the 'orientation paragraph'.

Layout of newspaper reports

1 Choose another well-known story and plan three paragraphs to make it into a newspaper report. Copy the following plan and fill in the details for your chosen story:

Orientation paragraph:
Who? What? Where? When? Why?

Main story paragraph:
All the information about the story with details and possibly quotes from people involved.

Re-orientation paragraph:
What has happened as a result of the main story.

2 Newspaper reports usually have an exciting or interesting headline (title) to help engage the reader.
There are different types of headlines:
- **Straight headlines** (these simply relate to the main topic of the story).
  Boy Finds New Creature
- **Question headlines** (these are often statements followed by a question mark and different to normal questions).
  New creature discovered similar to a cat?
- **Quotation headlines** (these are quoted speech).
  Boy says "I'm going to be famous"
- **Feature headlines** (these are often for unusual or amusing stories and don't give a whole meaning – they are intriguing). *Bat-like-cat Creature Found.*

Write a headline for your planned newspaper report.

Helpful hints

The **paragraphs** in the newspaper report help guide the reader through the story. As the plan shows, the final paragraph explains what happens as a result of the story and about the future for the people involved.
All newspaper reports have a similar set of features:
- **headline** – this is used to capture the reader's interest.
- **columns** – newspapers are written in narrow columns to make it easier to read. It also creates an easily recognisable structure for the reader and also helps to make the organisation on a page easier for the editor.
- **photographs** and **captions** – photos are used to show the characters/objects/places involved in the stories. These have captions to explain what the picture is.

A newspaper report

New creature similar to a cat?

Last night, Mateo Aguas (aged 10) found an amazing creature in the woods at the bottom of his garden, in the Calvillo. Scientists have yet to name the creature, but they have confirmed it has never been seen before.

Mateo Aguas was the normal boy until last night, when he made a discovery that is sure to make him famous. He was out walking in the woods at the bottom of his garden, when he heard a noise. This noise caused him to stop and find out what it was.

"It was weird," Mateo told our reporter, "It was like nothing I've ever seen before. It was like something

from a movie!"
The creature, which has yet to be named, has one pair of legs, which it uses to walk upright, and two more pairs of arms. It is covered in thick, short brown fur. Its face is exceptionally friendly looking, with a pair of large, baby-like eyes, and two bat-like ears. These waggle when it is happy. The creature seems to like being stroked and purrs loudly much like a cat.

"When I asked it if it wanted to come home with me," Mateo explained, "it pointed at my backpack. I'm sure it understood what I said."

The creature is now in protective custody. Mateo's mother, Mrs Maria Aguas, discovered it in Mateo's bedroom late last night. She called the authorities and they took it away. Mateo is now being interviewed by a team of scientists. The wood at the back of his house has been cordoned off, while search teams investigate and look for more of the creatures.

Word play

1 To make the headlines understandable, punctuation has to be used carefully. For example:

- **quotation marks** need to be shown around quotation headlines.
- **exclamation mark** needs to be used to show word play.
- **question mark** needs to be at the end of a question headline.
- **commas** need to be used if two clauses are used within a headline or if a list is given. For example, *Sun, sea and sand.*

Write a headline for your planned story from page 117 that requires:

a quotation marks
b an exclamation mark
c a question mark
d alliteration
e commas in a list.

Talk Partners

Read your headlines to a partner. Which one do they like best and why? Can they suggest any improvements to any of your headlines to make them even better?

Helpful hints

Headline writers can have lots of fun playing with words to make humorous and clever headlines:

- puns – this is when a sentence can have two meanings. For example, *Cinders rises from the ashes*. This means both that Cinderella rises from the depths of despair, and that cinders are what end up in the fire when it has burned.
- letter play – writers can change a letter to give a word a double meaning. For example, *Rip of a Lifetime!*
- alliteration – using the same letter sound at the start of words gives an interesting effect. For example, *Spending Time in Sea, Sun and Sand.*
- rhyme – when two words in the headline rhyme such as *Blue Crew*

Write headlines for the following well-known stories using the different techniques. Try to use a different technique for each story headline.

a Cinderella
b The Three Billy Goats Gruff
c Little Red Riding Hood
d The newspaper report on page 118

Try this

I can use different adjectives to make my writing more interesting.

Using adjectives

1 For each of these words, use a thesaurus to help you identify five alternative words to show the varying degrees of intensity of the adjective. The first one has been done for you.

a angry
annoyed, irritated, cross, fuming, furious

b fast

c good

d happy

e sad

Now put each set of words into alphabetical order.

Helpful hints

Adjectives are describing words and can be chosen to show the intensity of something. For example, rather than just hot you could use *warm, roasting* or *molten*.

2 Re-write the following sentences, replacing the adjectives shown in red with an alternative adjective meaning something similar but with a different intensity. Use a thesaurus to help you.

a The slow car drove down the rough road.

b The happy teacher smiled at the clever child.

c The warm sun shone down on the cold water.

Monster trouble

Once, during Anglo-Saxon times, there was a monster living near the city of Cushan in Fiendland. The people who lived in the city were scared of the monster and they left food out for it, so it didn't attack them.

One day Johan, a brave, courageous woman from the nearby city of Fushan came. The people of Cushan told her about their troubles and she spoke to them in a clear and **authoritative** voice, helping to stop their anxiety immediately.

"Let me see this **creature** for myself," she said. She stayed up all night and watched for the **beast**. As the dark hours ticked by, every shadow, every sound made the woman's senses heighten further. Just after 2 am, she heard a noise. As she stared into the blackness, she saw the creature land on a house and a boy and his father came running out. The monster grabbed the young boy and dragged him away.

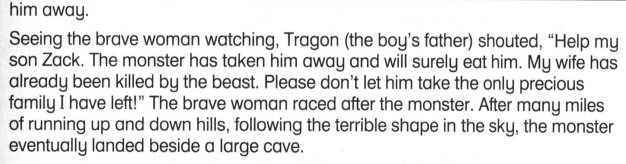

Glossary

authoritative: confident and commanding respect

creature: an animal, rather than a human being

beast: an animal that is usually large and dangerous

Seeing the brave woman watching, Tragon (the boy's father) shouted, "Help my son Zack. The monster has taken him away and will surely eat him. My wife has already been killed by the beast. Please don't let him take the only precious family I have left!" The brave woman raced after the monster. After many miles of running up and down hills, following the terrible shape in the sky, the monster eventually landed beside a large cave.

As Johan approached the dark cave on top of the mountain she saw that the monster was outside and had put the boy down, ready to eat him. The woman ran up and drew her sword. The monster snarled, taken by surprise. He leapt forward but she was too quick for him and cut its head off! She picked up the limp and exhausted Zack and ran back to the city.

Zack was so happy at being saved and Tragon so grateful that his son had been brought back safely that he asked Johan to marry him that very day. It wasn't long before she was made Mayor of Cushan!

I can use connectives in my writing.

I can make short notes from an extract.

Finding key points

a Read the story on page 121. Identify and write down the connectives used.

b For each connective, write down whether it is a sub-ordinating or co-ordinating connective.

c Add some examples of your own to the list.

Talk Partners

With a partner, identify the key points in the story on page 121 and make brief notes using the headings:

- why is it happening?
- where is this happening?
- when is it happening?
- what is happening?
- who is involved?

Helpful hints

A **connective** is a word or phrase that links two parts of a sentence together. The different types of connectives can be used at the beginning or middle of a sentence:

- **co-ordinating connectives** to join two clauses independent and of equal importance to one other, such as *and, but, or*
- **sub-ordinating connectives** link a main clause with a dependent clause, such as *if, so, although, because.*

2 In pairs, take the role of a reporter and Johan. The reporter asks Johan questions to find out how she felt during and after her adventure. For example:

- Why did you visit Cushan at the beginning?
- Did you believe the story the people of Cushan told you?
- How did you feel when you were waiting for the monster to appear?

Make brief notes of Johan's responses to your questions. Now swap roles. This time, one of you is the reporter and the other is Zack, the boy who was rescued. The reporter asks Zack questions and makes notes of his responses. For example:

- Why did you come out of your house in the night?
- What happened to your mother?
- How did you feel when the monster flew off with you into the sky?

Sentences

Helpful hints

There are three main types of sentence:
- **simple** – these include a subject (person/object the sentence is about) and a verb (action).
  They are a complete thought on their own:
      Ted   waited for the bus.
   (subject) (verb)
- **compound** – these are made up of two independent clauses (or complete sentences) and joined by a connective:
  Ted waited for the bus, but the bus did not come.
          (clause 1)   (connective) (clause 2)
- **complex** – these are made up of an independent clause (the main clause) and a dependent clause that would not make sense on its own. They are joined by connectives:
  When he had waited for two hours, Ted realised the bus wasn't coming.
  (connective) (dependent clause)   (main clause)

To make your writing better, you need to ensure you use a range of different sentence types.

1 From the text on page 121, find and write a:
   a   simple sentence   b   compound sentence   c   complex sentence

2 Write an example of each of the following types of sentences and label which type each is:

   command   statement   exclamation

3 Write these complex sentences and underline the main clause in each:
   a   Even though the train was late, Oscar got to his appointment on time.
   b   The soldiers were marching in line, even though the crowds were shouting loudly.
   c   The children were playing happily because they had toys to play with.

I can write newspaper-style reports.

I can find the key points in a report.

Writing a newspaper report

1 Read the story on page 121 again. Create a paragraph plan.

a   Write the key points you discussed with your talk partner on page 122 under the following headings:
  * orientation paragraph
  * main story paragraph
  * re-orientation paragraph.

b   Use your notes from activity 2 on page 122 to add any quotes to your paragraphs. For example, this note might be added to the main story paragraph: *"I thought I would never see my family again when the monster grabbed me"* said Zack, the son of Tragon.

c   Decide and write down a headline for the report using the ideas from pages 117 and 119 about headlines.

Writing presentation

Write your newspaper report, using your plan from activity 1. A newspaper is written in columns with the headline at the top. Remember to use joined-up handwriting throughout. Afterwards, check through your report and underline any words that are spelt incorrectly. Write these words in your spelling journal and practise spelling them.

Editing my writing

1 Read your newspaper report from page 124.

   a   Underline any verbs you have used. Write them as a list.

   b   Can you change these for more powerful verbs so as to have a greater effect on your reader?

2 Read through your report again and highlight any words you have used more than once.

   a   Can you think of alternatives for these? Make a list of the words you have overused and the alternative words you have thought of.

3 Put your new verbs and words from activities 1 and 2 into your report. Read through it again and check you have included:

- a range of different sentences (simple, compound and complex)
- a range of connectives to link the clauses in your sentences.

Helpful hints

Editing is an essential part of the writing process as it allows you, as the writer, to reflect on the words you have written and think about how they could be improved.

Using powerful verbs can make a big difference to your writing as they add description by showing the intensity of the verb. For example, *shouted* instead of *said*, or *tiptoed* instead of *walked*.

Did you know?

Newspaper editors have the responsibility of deciding which news stories are printed in the paper each day. The Editor in Chief of a newspaper is responsible for all aspects of the newspaper including the content of the paper, who they employ to write the stories and financial decisions. The Managing Editor attends to the day to day running of the newsroom. It is their responsibility to get the paper out each day and make sure it is the best it can be.

The Accident

Adric had his hand X-rayed after an accident at work yesterday. He was carefully drilling holes to fix the hinges on a wooden gate outside. Suddenly the electrical cord of the drill got caught on the edge of the gate and the drill accidently jerked out of his hand.

Then the point of the drill broke off on the gate and it shot into his other hand. After the doctor looked at the X-ray, she quickly removed the bit of drill from Adric's hand and finally stitched up the hole.

Looking at your bones

Doctors use special X-ray machines to take photographs of your bones. This is an X-ray photograph of Adric's hand. You can see the bones in his hand and a piece of metal drill which is stuck near his bones.

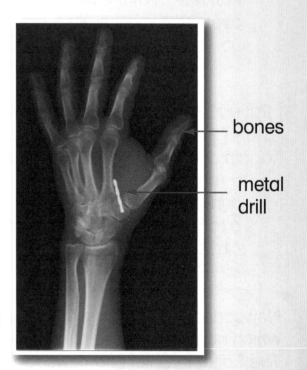

bones

metal drill

Using adverbs

Talk Partners

Read the report on page 126 with a partner and discuss the key points.
What features make you want to read the report? Why?

Helpful hints

An **adverb** is a word that changes the meaning of an adjective, verb or another adverb by adding further details about time, manner or place:

- **adverbs of time:** *yesterday, tomorrow, frequently*
- **adverbs of manner:** *accidentally, cheerfully, gently*
- **adverbs of place:** *above, here, towards.*

1 Read this sentence from the report on page 126:

Adric had his hand x-rayed after an accident at work yesterday.

In this sentence the word *yesterday* is the adverb and it shows the time, as it tells us **when** Adric had the accident. Copy the table below.

Adverbs of time	Adverbs of manner	Adverbs of place

Read through the rest of the report and identify the adverbs, writing them into the correct column of the table.

Talk Partners

Share your completed table with a partner and check that you have both identified and sorted them correctly.

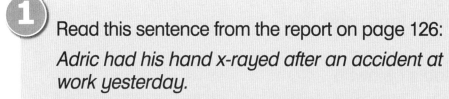

Find the sentences that the adverbs are included in within the text on page 126.

a Read the sentence as it is written, with the adverb included.
b Re-read the sentence, leaving the adverb out of the sentence.
c Discuss how the adverb gives extra information to the sentence and why it is important to use these in your writing.

Verbs

1 Copy and complete these sentences, choosing the correct form of the verb 'to be'.

a I _____ 9 years old on my next birthday.
b We _____ excited about our trip tomorrow.
c She _____ a girl.
d It _____ raining yesterday and _____ raining tomorrow as well.

2 Write three of your own sentences using the verb 'to be' in the
a past tense, b present tense and c future tense.

3 Copy and complete the table below:

	Past	Present	Future
to play	I _____ he _____ she _____ it _____ we _____ you _____ they _____	I _____ he _____ she _____ it _____ we _____ you _____ they _____	I _____ he _____ she _____ it _____ we _____ you _____ they _____
to build	I _____ he _____ she _____ it _____ we _____ you _____ they _____	I _____ he _____ she _____ it _____ we _____ you _____ they _____	I _____ he _____ she _____ it _____ we _____ you _____ they _____
to run	I _____ he _____ she _____ it _____ we _____ you _____ they _____	I _____ he _____ she _____ it _____ we _____ you _____ they _____	I _____ he _____ she _____ it _____ we _____ you _____ they _____

I know how to use the past, present and future tenses of verbs.

More verbs

1

	Past	Present	Future
to have	I **had** he/she/it **had** we/you **had**	I **have** he/she/it **has** we/you **have**	I **will have** he/she/it **will have** we/you **will have**

a   Write 6 sentences using the verb 'to have' (2 in the past, 2 in the present and 2 in the future tense).
b   Mark each one to show which tense you have written it in.

2   Draw a verb table (like the one above) to demonstrate the past, present and future tenses of the following verbs:
a   to stand
b   to cry

3   Write a sentence for each tense of the verb in activity 2.

What have I learnt?

You have been reading and writing newspaper reports and have identified the key features of these. Answer these questions:
● What are the key components of a newspaper report?
● What is usually included in the opening paragraph of a newspaper report?
● Give 3 examples of different ways to write a headline.
● How do commas help to give meaning to a sentence?
● How do adjectives vary in terms of their intensity? Give an example.

Unit 9 Imagery in poetry

Similes

Examples of similes:

- He was as tall as a giraffe!

- He was as small as a mouse!

- The moon was like a round cheese.
- She was as fast as a rocket.
- The snake was as green as the grass.
- The kangaroo bounced like a ball.

1 Similes use the words 'as' or 'like' to compare two things.
Write similes for the following sentence starters:
- a The lion was as angry as …
- b The car sped like a …
- c The man trudged as slowly as a …
- d Giraffes are as tall as …
- e The stars were like …

2 Choose one of your sentences above and draw a picture to illustrate the comparison between the two objects. Share your picture with a partner and ask them what they think the simile is.

3 Write your own similes to compare the following pairs of items:

a Frog and hair gel. For example, *The frog was as slimy as hair gel.*

b An aeroplane and a rocket

c The sun and a plate

d A rock and a basketball

4 Write three similes that compare two different objects.

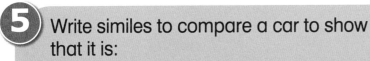

5 Write similes to compare a car to show that it is:

a slow
b fast
c red
d old
e new

Alliteration in poetry

Betty Botter

Betty Botter bought some butter
But she said the butter's bitter,
"If I put it in my batter
It will make my batter bitter,
But a bit of better butter
Will make my batter better."

So she bought some better butter
Better than the bitter butter,
And she put it in her batter
And her batter was not bitter,
So 'twas better Betty Botter
Bought a bit of better butter.

From Mother Goose

Helpful hints

Alliteration is when the same letter or sound is at the beginning of two words that are next to each other or closely connected to each other, such as *the whispering wind* or *rose rapidly*. Poets use alliteration to create emotion in their writing. Often it can help the poem to flow better so that the reader understands the tone and rhythm of the poem.

Alliteration

Talk Partners

Take turns, with a partner, to read a verse of the poem on page 132. Answer these questions:
  a Is it hard to read? Explain your answer.
  b How does the alliteration make the poem funny?
  c Did you enjoy the poem? Why or why not?

1

a With a partner, write three similes that you could use to describe butter. For example, *The butter is as yellow as the sun.*

b Write alliteration examples to go with the following words:
  • leopards
  • sister
  • sun
  • bunnies
  • fish

Write the first two lines of your own poem using alliteration. For example:

Try this

Little Larry
Little Larry learnt lots of lessons ...

I can build words from other words with similar meanings.

Playing with words

1 Look at the word *butter* in the poem on page 132.

 a How has it been changed throughout the poem by only changing one letter?

 b What type of letter has been changed (e.g. vowel or consonant?)

 c Why would this not work if you changed one of the other letters in the word?

2 Use a dictionary to help you find two words with similar meanings for each example below. Next to each word, write the definition.

 a super

 b micro

 c under

 d out

Can you explain the way that the words in each example are similar in meaning?

Helpful hints

Some words can be built from other words with similar meanings. For example **medic** is a person who cares for people when they are ill, while **medic**ine is something that is given to people when they are ill. The meaning is similar but the word has been built on to mean something else.

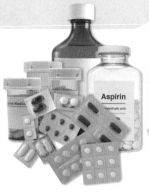

Rhyming patterns in poetry

Fireworks

They rise like sudden fiery flowers
That burst upon the night,
Then fall to earth in burning showers
Of crimson, blue, and white.

Like buds too wonderful to name,
Each miracle unfolds,
And Catherine-wheels begin to flame
Like whirling marigolds.

Rockets and Roman candles make
An orchard of the sky.
Whence magic trees their petals shake
Upon each gazing eye.

By James Reeves

Glossary

crimson: a deep red colour, almost purple

marigolds: a plant, like a daisy that has yellow or orange flowers

whence: from where

Roman candles: a firework that ejects one or more stars

Catherine wheels: a circular spinning firework

I can understand how mood is created through words.

I can explore how imagery is used in poetry.

Rhythm and rhyme

1 Identify the three similes used in the poem on page 135.

2 a Write down the words that rhyme in the poem.
b What do you notice about the rhyme scheme?

Talk Partners

Take it in turns to read the poem aloud to a partner. When reading, make sure that you:

- use the punctuation to help you make clear the meaning of the poem
- use the line breaks as pauses to break up the words
- stop briefly between the verses
- emphasise the rhymes as they appear in the poem
- discuss what impact the rhyming words have on the enjoyment of the poem.
  a Do the rhyming words change the way you read it? If so, how?
  b Does it create a clear rhythm?
  c What effect do the similes have on the pictures created in the listener's head?

Helpful hints

A **rhyme scheme** is the pattern of rhyme between lines in a poem. For example, in a four line poem or verse, the following rhyme patterns can occur:

- **AABB** (the first two lines rhyme with each other and the second two lines rhyme with each other)
- **ABAB** (the first and third lines rhyme with each other and the second and fourth lines rhyme with each other)
- **ABCB** (only the second and fourth lines rhyme)

Onomatopoeia

Helpful hints

Onomatopoeic words are words that sound like the thing that they represent, for example *beep*. They are often used in poetry as they are very descriptive. They can be used to introduce animal characters without saying the name of the character, such as *Quack* shows there is a duck, but this does not need explaining!

Examples of onomatopoeiac words:
zap   boom
jingle   clang   pop
hiss   smash
splatter   rustle

The old car

The old car
pops
creaks
hisses
and finally splutters into life;
But then the sound of
a jingle
a crackle
a boom
and finally a smash
The car was no more.

Did you know?

The poem Beowulf is the oldest surviving epic Old English poem. It consists of 3182 alliterative long lines and dates back to Anglo-Saxon times. The poem is now housed in the British Library in London after it was nearly destroyed by a fire in 1731 in Ashburnham House in the city.

Onomatopoeic words

1 Read the poem on page 137. It is simple in form as it uses the words to create the mood.

Write a paragraph explaining what you understand the poem to mean. Include the following in your answer:

- What does the first part of the poem show? How do the words used create this idea? For example, the word *creaks* shows that the car is not making the sound that a car should and emphasises how old it is.
- What happens in the middle of the poem? What words help you to understand this?
- What do you understand by the final noises and lines of the poem?

2 Pick a subject from the bubble below. Choose three onomatopoeic words from the Helpful hints box on page 137 and use them to write your own short poem about the subject.

breakfast   school   breaktime

playing in the park

Use this structure to help you:

Line 1:   introduce the subject. For example, *The old car ...*
Lines 2–4:   list words to create a mood
Lines 5–6:   show a change in what is happening. For example, *the car comes to life and then new sounds are heard*
Lines 7–9:   list words to create the new mood
Lines 10–11: the final lines to show what happened at the end. For example, *the car was no more.*

Planning, writing and performing poetry

1
Think back to the language examples you have used in this unit:
- Similes • Alliteration • Rhyme • Onomatopoeic words.

Plan a short poem that has a clear rhyming pattern.

Follow these steps to help you create your poem:

a Choose a subject
b Brainstorm the words you are going to use
c Decide what language features to use
d Plan the lines using the language feature you have chosen
e Choose a rhyming scheme (e.g. AABB, ABAB, ABCB)
f Decide where the planned lines will go
g Write rhyming words that will work with the lines you
   have already written.

Writing presentation

Write your poem and then read it aloud
to a friend. Listen to any feedback and
make changes that you want.

2
Perform your poem to a larger audience
(a group or the class).

What have
I learnt?

You have been studying the imagery in poetry and
fiction texts and identifying the ways that authors and poets
create pictures in your mind. See if you can answer the following questions:

- Can you write an example of a simile?
- How can figurative language create mood? Give an example in your answer.
- Can you write an example of alliteration?
- Name three different rhyming patterns that can be used in poetry.
- What are onomatopoeic words? Give three examples in your answer.

Fiction

Read the text and answer ALL the questions that follow.

Marlin Maxton knew that all dinosaurs were extinct. He was sure of it. Of course there were still birds – there were plenty of those – but the big dinosaurs, the really big ones, they were gone and nothing like them would ever be seen again.

That's what Marlin thought, right up until the night he visited his uncle's workshop.

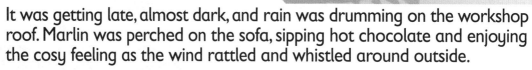

It was getting late, almost dark, and rain was drumming on the workshop roof. Marlin was perched on the sofa, sipping hot chocolate and enjoying the cosy feeling as the wind rattled and whistled around outside.

Uncle Gus was always making things – fixing things together and coming up with strange inventions. Some people thought he was foolish – and it's true he was a bit scruffy and more than a bit forgetful – but Marlin knew he was really very clever.

On this particular night Uncle Gus had the parts from a very old engine laid out on the floor, waiting to be repaired. He was sitting completely still, thinking about something (something complicated, probably) when suddenly he looked up.

"School trip to the museum tomorrow, Marlin?" he said. "I wonder if you'll see old Protos?"

He took a sip of his drink and his eyes twinkled at Marlin through the rising steam.

"Protos? Who's that?"

"Who's that?" he laughed. "Did I never tell you?"

Marlin shook his head.

"No."

"That's odd…" frowned Uncle Gus – and he leaned forward. "Never mind, I'll tell you now. Years ago, when I was young, I thought Protos was the best thing in the museum. He's a metal dinosaur."
A gust of wind rattled the workshop.

The Secret Dinosaur: Giants Awake! By N S Blackman

1 What is Marlin going to be doing the next day? (1)

2 From the description of Uncle Gus, why do you think some people thought he was foolish? (1)

3 **a** Has Marlin seen a real dinosaur?
  b How do you know? (2)

4 When Uncle Gus says 'That's odd…' what is he referring to? (1)

5 **a** Find the line *That's what Marlin thought, right up until the night he visited his uncle's workshop.* What does this mean? (1)

  b What do you think Uncle Gus is going to tell Marlin about the dinosaur at the museum? (1)

6 The author has called the main character Marlin Maxton. What is this an example of? Write one answer.
  a alliteration
  b simile
  c rhyming

7 Find and write the two words the author uses to show that Uncle Gus is old. (2)

8 You have read the extract from the story about Marlin. Your task is to write the next part of the story when Marlin visits the museum.
Before you write, think about: (8)

What he saw	What exhibits will Marlin see at the museum? Which did he like best?
What was special about Protos	Does he come to life? Is he a real dinosaur? Does everyone see him as a real dinosaur?
Events that happened	What happens on the way to the museum? What happens at the museum? What happens at the end of the day?

Fiction

Read the text and answer ALL the questions that follow.

Teeny Tiny Dino Fun!

Yesterday morning, around 10 am, people in Summerville were astonished to see what appeared to be a baby Tyrannosaurus-Rex hiding in the bushes near the town hall.

The first person to see the creature was the town mayor, John Hopkins, who said, "I heard a rustling in the bushes and when I looked more closely, I saw a tiny little creature that looked exactly like a Tyrannosaurus-Rex!" Mr Hopkins did not want to disturb the creature in case it was dangerous. By the time the police arrived a huge crowd had gathered to see the creature. The police called the animal sanctuary.

Janet Jones from the animal sanctuary collected the mini-dino and told us, "We have secured the creature and taken it to our centre so that we can try to identify it.

"I can honestly say that I have never seen anything like it before. It looks exactly like a Tyrannosaurus-Rex but is only as big as a mouse. Incredible!"

The creature is being well cared for at present. Interest of experts from all around the world has been aroused, many of whom are flying to Summerville to see this incredible creature. The question is, where did it come from?

1 Write down two people who came into contact with the dinosaur. (4)

2 Do you think that the Mayor was wise not to touch the dinosaur?
Give reasons for your answer using information from the text. (2)

3 What is the name of the town mayor? (1)

4 Who is looking after the creature now?
Choose one answer from below. (1)
a   experts   b animal sanctuary
c   The Mayor   d Police

5 The author has used quotes in the newspaper report.
Why has he done this? Choose two answers from below. (2)
a   To fill up the space.
b   To show the reactions and thoughts of the people involved.
c   To add variety to the text by using speech to describe what happened.
d   To show the thoughts of the dinosaur.

6 Find and write an example of alliteration used in the text. (1)

7 Find and write an example of a simile used in the text. (1)

8 Identify the onomatopoeic word used in the text. (1)

9 Write your own newspaper report (7)
about a discovery.
This could be about a real animal or an imaginary animal.
Before you write, think about:

Headline	How will you grab your reader's attention?
Key information	Who finds the animal? What is the animal? Why was it where it was? How was it discovered? When was it found?
The future	What has happened as a result of the discovery?